First World War
and Army of Occupation
War Diary
France, Belgium and Germany

19 DIVISION
Divisional Troops
88 Brigade Royal Field Artillery
1 July 1915 - 31 December 1918

WO95/2067/5

The Naval & Military Press Ltd
www.nmarchive.com
Published in association with The National Archives

Published by

The Naval & Military Press Ltd

Unit 10 Ridgewood Industrial Park,

Uckfield, East Sussex,

TN22 5QE England

Tel: +44 (0) 1825 749494

www.naval-military-press.com

www.nmarchive.com

This diary has been reprinted in facsimile from the original. Any imperfections are inevitably reproduced and the quality may fall short of modern type and cartographic standards.

Contents

Miscellaneous	XIXth Divisional Artillery Instructions For Relief No 11.	19/11/1915	19/11/1915
Heading	19th Div 88th Bde: R.F.A. Vol: 5 Dec 1915		
War Diary	Bas Hamel	01/12/1915	04/12/1915
War Diary	La Couture X. 4.b 8.6	05/12/1915	31/12/1915
Heading	88th Bde: R.F.A. Vol 7		
War Diary	La Couture	01/01/1916	31/01/1916
War Diary	Bas Hamel J. 31. C. 2.8	01/02/1916	17/02/1916
War Diary	Rue de Garadis Layantie M. 4. C. 1.1	18/02/1916	18/02/1916
War Diary	Laventie M. 4. C. 1.1	18/02/1916	29/02/1916
Heading	19 88 R F A Vol 8		
War Diary	Laventie	01/03/1916	31/03/1916
Heading	88th Bde. RFA Vol: 6		
War Diary	Laventie	01/04/1916	19/04/1916
War Diary	Bas Hamel Delette.	20/04/1916	30/04/1916
War Diary	Delette	01/05/1916	10/05/1916
War Diary	Belloy	11/05/1916	30/05/1916
War Diary	Caours	01/06/1916	11/06/1916
War Diary	Belloy	12/06/1916	13/06/1916
War Diary	Behencourt	14/06/1916	30/06/1916
Heading	Headquarters. 88th Brigade. R.F.A. July 1916		
War Diary	Dernacourt	01/07/1916	31/07/1916
Miscellaneous	34th Division.	18/07/1916	18/07/1916
Heading	88th Brigade Royal Field Artillery August 1916		
War Diary	N. 13. C. 2. 9 Trench Ref 1/10000 Wytschaete Edition 3 D	01/08/1916	31/08/1916
War Diary		01/09/1916	30/09/1916
War Diary		01/10/1916	31/10/1916
War Diary		01/11/1916	30/11/1916
War Diary		01/12/1916	31/12/1916
War Diary		01/01/1917	31/01/1917
War Diary		01/02/1917	28/02/1917
War Diary		01/03/1917	31/03/1917
War Diary	Polincove (2nd Army Training Area)	01/04/1917	21/04/1917
War Diary	La Clytte	22/04/1917	30/04/1917
War Diary	La Clytte	01/05/1917	01/05/1917
War Diary	Lille Gate Ypres	02/05/1917	03/05/1917
War Diary	Railway Dug-Outs at I 21 C O 8	04/05/1917	08/05/1917
War Diary	Railway Dug-Outs.	09/05/1917	11/05/1917
War Diary	Nr Westoutre	12/05/1917	25/05/1917
War Diary	La Clytte N 7 C 3 5.	26/05/1917	31/05/1917
War Diary	La Clytte	01/06/1917	03/06/1917
War Diary	Farm at N 3 B 4 2 1/2	04/06/1917	09/06/1917
War Diary	Beggars's Rest Hedge N 6 D 3 1/2 6 1/2	10/06/1917	19/06/1917
War Diary	M 8 C 0 4.	20/06/1917	27/06/1917
War Diary	N 18 A 2 5.	28/06/1917	30/06/1917
War Diary	N 18 A 20 50	01/07/1917	10/07/1917
War Diary	N 18 A 2 5	11/07/1917	13/07/1917
War Diary	Grand Bois.	14/07/1917	31/07/1917
War Diary	Grand Bois.	01/08/1917	31/08/1917
War Diary	Merris	01/09/1917	05/09/1917
War Diary	Siege Farm N 16 c 2 9	06/09/1917	20/09/1917
War Diary	Siege Farm	20/09/1917	30/09/1917
War Diary	Siege Farm N 16 C 2.9	01/10/1917	17/11/1917
War Diary	Lock 7	18/11/1917	30/11/1917
War Diary	Lock 7 I 32 b 7 3	01/12/1917	13/12/1917

War Diary	N 7 a 7 8	14/12/1917	21/12/1917
War Diary	G 36 a 7 8	22/12/1917	31/12/1917
War Diary	Camp "B" Rocquigny	01/01/1918	02/01/1918
War Diary	K 36 a 6 0	03/01/1918	31/01/1918
War Diary	K 36 a 6 0	01/02/1918	28/02/1918
Heading	88th Brigade R.F.A. March 1918		
War Diary	Ytres	01/03/1918	04/03/1918
War Diary	Q 3 d. 14	05/03/1918	21/03/1918
War Diary	Neuville	22/03/1918	22/03/1918
War Diary	Bourjonval	22/03/1918	25/03/1918
War Diary	Herissart	26/03/1918	28/03/1918
War Diary	Berteaucourt	29/03/1918	31/03/1918
Heading	19th Divisional Artillery. 88th Brigade R.F.A. ::: April 1918		
War Diary	Boubers-Sur-Canche	01/04/1918	05/04/1918
War Diary	Ravelsberg Camp S. 17 c 5.8	06/04/1918	12/04/1918
War Diary	Locre	13/04/1918	27/04/1918
War Diary	L-21 c	28/04/1918	30/04/1918
War Diary	Champagne	01/05/1918	18/05/1918
War Diary	Dampierre-Sur-Moivre	20/05/1918	28/05/1918
War Diary	Bisseuil	29/05/1918	29/05/1918
War Diary	Sarcy	30/05/1918	30/05/1918
War Diary	Chamuzy	31/05/1918	01/06/1918
War Diary	Bullen	02/06/1918	21/06/1918
War Diary	Bannes	22/06/1918	30/06/1918
Operation(al) Order(s)	Order No. 84		
War Diary		02/07/1918	02/07/1918
War Diary	Merck-St-Lieven	03/07/1918	31/07/1918
War Diary	Febvin Palfart.	01/08/1918	05/08/1918
War Diary	Sheet 36a SE 1/40,000 Bois Des Dame.	06/08/1918	06/08/1918
War Diary	Sheet 36a SE 1/40,000 Chateau L'Abbaye O 35 c 3 4	07/08/1918	22/08/1918
War Diary	Bowers Retreat. W 7 a 10 15	23/08/1918	31/08/1918
War Diary	W 14 b 2 8	01/09/1918	01/09/1918
War Diary	X 2 a 5 8	02/09/1918	30/09/1918
War Diary	Bethune	01/10/1918	04/10/1918
War Diary	Ligny-Le-Grand	05/10/1918	11/10/1918
War Diary	N 30 d 5 5	11/10/1918	30/10/1918
War Diary	Outrebois.	01/12/1918	31/12/1918

WO95/2067

19 Div - 88 Bde

RFA

Aug 1915 - Dec 1918

(Nov 1918 missing)

19TH DIVISION

88TH BRIGADE R.F.A.

AUG 1915 - DEC 1918

19

87th Bde: R.F.A.

Vol: 7

19th Division

88th Bde: R.F.A.

Vol: I

August. 15

Dec '18

Instructions regarding War Diaries and Intelligence Summaries are contained in F. S. Regs., Part II. and the Staff Manual respectively. Title Pages will be prepared in manuscript.

WAR DIARY
or
INTELLIGENCE SUMMARY
(Erase heading not required.)

Army Form C. 2118.

Place	Date	Hour	Summary of Events and Information	Remarks and references to Appendices
LE VERT BOIS	1.7.15		Remain in billets. Shells noticed bursting over [illegible] about 3 pm	
	2.7.15		Remain in billets.	
	3.7.15		Remain in billets.	
	4.7.15		" "	
	5.7.15		Bde inspected by Gen. Sir James Willcox. March 3 p.m. to new billets at PARADIS. Maj. Cox & 2/Lt Herzog attached to 13th F.A. Bde	
PARADIS	6.7.15		Remain in billets. Lt Campbell & 2/Lt Macardle attached to 9th F.A. Bde.	
	7.7.15		Remain in billets. News of Warsaw	
	8.7.15		" " " Trenches captured in front of Hooge by [illegible]	
	9.7.15		" " "	
	10.7.15		" " "	
	11.7.15		" " "	
	12.7.15		" " "	
	13.7.15		" " "	
	16.7.15		The Colonel accompanied Gen. Stuart round the infantry posts of the BOUTDEVILLE System	
	17.8.15		Remain in billets.	
	18.8.15		Horse show. Brig. Gen. Lawrie and Gen. Stuart attend. A great success.	
	19.8.15		Remain in billets.	
	20.8.15		Tactical Exercise. Reconnoitre gun positions in second line of defence. CROIX BARBÉE System. Colonel attached to 18th F.A. Bde.	
	21.8.15		Remain in billets.	

1875 Wt. W593/826 1,000,000 4/15 J.B.C. & A. A.D.S.S./Forms/C. 2118.

Instructions regarding War Diaries and Intelligence Summaries are contained in F. S. Regs., Part II. and the Staff Manual respectively. Title Pages will be prepared in manuscript.

WAR DIARY
or
INTELLIGENCE SUMMARY
(Erase heading not required.)

Army Form C. 2118

Place	Date	Hour	Summary of Events and Information	Remarks and references to Appendices
~~22.8.15~~ PARADIS	22.8.15		Remain in billets.	
	23.8.15		Receive orders that we are going to relieve 22nd F.A. Bde HQ at X17d93 Combined BETHUNE map 1/40000.	
	24.8.15		~~night~~ One section per battery is to relieve one section per battery 22nd Bde. Bde HQrs nominally move up but are not to take command till 27th inst. Four (4) sections move in 9.30 pm in place of sections of 104th 105th 106th & 58th Btys.	
	25.8.15		2nd section per battery 88th Bde except A/88 relieve corresponding sections of 22nd Bde. 9.30 p.m.	
	26.8.15		Third sections of 104th 105th 106th Btys move out 9.30 p.m.	
	27.8.15		Relief completed. Divisional Arty divided into groups. Northern group 88th Bde. D86. B86 D87. Southern group. 2 batteries 86th Bde. 3 batteries 87th Bde. To take over new zone 10 a.m. 28th inst. HQRS 22nd FA Bde move out.	
	28.8.15	10 am	Group system starts. D/88 Counter battery. D87. Enfilade battery. Batteries register their zones. Night 28/29 57th Bde infantry relieve 22nd & 20th Inf Bdes of 7th Div.	
	29.8.15		Batteries continue registration of zones. 57 Inf Bde distributed as follows. Rt Gloucesters Centre 10th Worcesters. Left Warwicks. 58th Bde hold line on right of 57th Bde and Ferozepore Bde, LAHORE DIVISION on left of 57th Bde.	
	30.8.15		Quiet day on our front. Batteries continue registration. Groups renamed. N Group IND 2 S Group IND I	
	31.8.15		Quiet day. Enemy bomb the IRCUTRA D salient with trench mortars. 12.30 a.m. A88 + B88 retaliate on COUR D'AVOUÉ	

G Campbell Lt
adj. 88th Bde

/21
7/21

19th Division

88th Bde: R.F.A.

Vol 2.

Sept. 15

Instructions regarding War Diaries and Intelligence Summaries are contained in F. S. Regs., Part II. and the Staff Manual respectively. Title Pages will be prepared in manuscript.

WAR DIARY
or
INTELLIGENCE SUMMARY
(Erase heading not required.)

Army Form C. 21[illegible]

Place	Date	Hour	Summary of Events and Information	Remarks and references to Appendices
Rue de Bois X17d.	1.9.15		Nothing of importance to report. Batteries continues registration & retaliated at the request of our infantry when required to do so.	
	2.9.15		A quiet day.	
	3.9.15		Enemy continually bomb ORCHARD SALIENT. Otherwise nothing of importance	
	4.9.15		Nothing of importance to report.	
	5.9.15		About 5-6 pm enemy fired about 30 15 cm HE at D36. The range was good but there were about 30% blind. No damage done.	
	6.9.15		First definite information of an attack to come. Report Center selected on the RUE DE CAILLOUX and order received to establish telephonic communication with this report center & batteries. Very little telephone wire available. Weather fine. Wind E.	
	7.9.15		Wires laid out from present HQ to Report center. Brief retaliation on enemy trenches	
	8.9.15		Weather still fine. Wind East. Work is being done on Report Center & communication improved. Order to provide bomb proof head cover for gun pits	
	9.9.15		Weather fine Wind E.	
	10.9.15		Work on telephonic communication & gun pits continues. German aeroplane brought down near BOIS DU BIEZ	
	11.9.15		Nothing of importance to report. D59 howitzer battery attached to IND 2 group	
	12.9.15		Very little firing. Trench mortars continue to bomb ORCHARD SALIENT. Very little ammunition allowed for retaliation	
	13.9.15		On night 13/14 57th Inf Bde relieved by 58th Inf Bde. ORCHARD SALIENT	

1875 Wt. W593/826 1,000,000 4/15 J.B.C. & A. A.D.S.S./Forms/C. 2118.

Instructions regarding War Diaries and Intelligence Summaries are contained in F. S. Regs., Part II. and the Staff Manual respectively. Title Pages will be prepared in manuscript.

WAR DIARY
or
INTELLIGENCE SUMMARY
(Erase heading not required.)

Army Form C. 2118

Place	Date	Hour	Summary of Events and Information	Remarks and references to Appendices
	13.9.15		heavily bombed from 11 p.m 13th - 2 a.m 14th. D88 reply without much effect but some HE from D89 howitzer battery appeared to silence the trench mortars. Observation haystack recently strengthened for B88. hit by shell & burnt down	
	14.9.15		Quiet day. Very little firing. Wind changes to S.W. in evening	
	15.9.15		Quiet day. Information recieved that	
	16.9.15 - 19.9.15		Very little shooting. D86 and C86 have the use of an aeroplane on the 19th for registering but did not accomplish much.	
	20.9.15		Weather still fine. Wind. E. The front is to be extended to RUE D'OUVERT S27c82. The front is now held as follows. Rt battalion IND2 A. 7th E. Lancs. Centre IND2 B. Royal Lancs. Left IND2 C South Lancs. Orders recieved that preliminary 4 days bombardment is to commence at 8 a.m. 21.9.15.	
	21.9.15		1st day of bombardment. German Artillery very quiet all day. Weather fine. Wind E. Results of bombardment good. HE (18pr) appears satisfactory except for a few air bursts. C88 had a gun put out of action by an explosion apparently in the cartridge in the bore. Causing a bulge.	
	22.9.15		2nd day of bombardment. Weather still fine. Wind E. German artillery again very quiet. A feint attack made by LAHORE Div on our left at 5 p.m. The idea being ~~that~~ to make the Germans man their front trenches & then shell them. This was not achieved as sufficient time was not given to allow of them manning the trenches. A similar feint has been arranged on our own front for tomorrow.	

1875 Wt. W593/826 1,000,000 4/15 J.B.C. & A. A.D.S.S./Forms/C. 2118.

Army Form C. 2118.

Instructions regarding War Diaries and Intelligence Summaries are contained in F. S. Regs., Part II. and the Staff Manual respectively. Title Pages will be prepared in manuscript.

WAR DIARY
or
INTELLIGENCE SUMMARY
(Erase heading not required.)

Place	Date	Hour	Summary of Events and Information	Remarks and references to Appendices
23.9.15	23.9.15		Bombardment Continued. At 3.30 p.m. a feint attack was made on enemy line between pt. S22 C45 and S22a41. A88 and B88 took part in this. At 3.30 pm fire was opened on enemy front trenches. At 3.35 p.m. a rocket was fired and artillery fire was lifted to second line trenches. Infantry cheered and showed their bayonets above the trenches. At 3.40 rapid fire was opened with guns & rifles at front line trenches for 3 minutes. It is improbable that the Germans were deceived. After the feint was over one German signalled "Wash out".	
	24.9.15		Fourth and last day of bombardment. HQ IND 2 moved to Advance report Centre at 4 p.m. Arrangements for 25th completed & final orders received except for the hour. Weather warm & dull. Wind uncertain.	
	25.9.15	4.30 a.m.	Zero time received. Gas attack to start at 5.50 a.m.	
		5.50 a.m.	Gas & smoke attack starts.	
		6.30 a.m.	News received that 2nd Div have taken 2 lines of German trenches. Thereupon the signal to attack was given for 58th Inf Bde. The next authentic news received is that the 2nd Div are back in their trenches and the 58th Inf Bde have lost heavily without ever reaching the German 1st line trench. During this period our artillery acted as follows. 5.5 a.m. - 6.20 a.m. a slow rate of fire was kept up by all batteries on enemy's front line trenches. At 6.30 a.m. D86, C86, A88 fired on selected works in rear of German lines.	

Instructions regarding War Diaries and Intelligence Summaries are contained in F. S. Regs., Part II. and the Staff Manual respectively. Title Pages will be prepared in manuscript.

WAR DIARY
or
INTELLIGENCE SUMMARY
(Erase heading not required.)

Army Form C. 2118

Place	Date	Hour	Summary of Events and Information	Remarks and references to Appendices
	25.9.15		After 6.30 a.m. practically all firing on our front ceased and the remainder of the day was quiet. During the morning gas shells were fired to the neighbourhood of LACOUTURE. C88 suffering one man evacuated to hospital.	
	26.9.15		During the night fire to the extent of 48 rounds per battery was kept up on german communication & rear trenches. Remainder of the day was quiet on our front. News received that the French had captured SOUCHEZ. At about 7.15 pm heavy firing broke out on our right in front of the 2nd Div. A large quantity of luminous rockets & flares were sent up by the enemy.	
	27.9.15		Night of 26-27th was quiet only 2 rds per gun being allowed for night firing. Urgent message was received during the morning ordering the most extreme economy as regards ammunition expenditure. A very quiet day.	
	28.9.15		During the morning some shells fell in B 88 gun position. One man was killed, 3 wounded and 1 horse killed. A few gas shells were also fired and caused inconvenience. Otherwise a very quiet day was passed.	
	29.9.15		Orders received that the 58th Inf Bde is to occupy its original front again; CANADIAN ORCHARD SALIENT (inclusive) - FARM CORNER. At the same time another Bde of INDIAN CORPS (SIRHIND) having come in on the right of 58th Inf Bde the 58th Bde Section is renamed INDIAN III. Zones of batteries revert to what they were before the bombardment. D86 retain the Salient. C86 still remain in the group.	

1875 Wt. W593/826 1,000,000 4/15 J.B.C. & A. A.D.S.S./Forms/C. 2118.

Army Form C. 2118

Instructions regarding War Diaries and Intelligence Summaries are contained in F. S. Regs., Part II. and the Staff Manual respectively. Title Pages will be prepared in manuscript.

WAR DIARY
or
INTELLIGENCE SUMMARY
(Erase heading not required.)

Place	Date	Hour	Summary of Events and Information	Remarks and references to Appendices
Adj. Rep. A.C. 30.9.15.	30.9.15		Situation remained unchanged. Very little firing on our front.	

A. Beal
Adjt. [illegible] Bde
R.F.A.

[illegible] Lt. Col

1875 Wt. W593/826 1,000,000 4/15 J.B.C. & A. A.D.S.S./Forms/C. 2118.

Officers Commanding Units,

Ind: II. Group.

With reference to instructions previously issued regarding night firing on selected localities, each being engaged every half-hour

Time	Battery	Target	No.of rounds
7.32½ p.m.	A 88	S 27d 36	2
7.35	B 88	S 22c 86	2
7.37½	C 88	RUE DE CAILLOUX	2
7.40	D 88	Fm De TOULLOTTE	2
7.42½	C 86	S 27d 95	2
7.45	D 86	RUE DE MARAIS	2
7.47½	A 88	S 28b 39	2
7.50	B 88	S 22b 6I	2
7.52½	C 88	Fm du Bois	2
7.55	D 88	Fm COUR D'AVOUE	2
7.57½	C 86	S 28d 3I	2
8.0	D 86	X roads VIOLAINES	2
8.2½	A 88	S 28d 55	2
8.5	B 88	S 22c 86	2
8.7½	C 88	RUE DE CAILLOUX	2
8.I0	D 88	Fm De TOULLOTTE	2
8.I2½	C 86	S 28d 97	2
8.I5	D 86	RUE DE MARAIS	2

and so on every half-hour i.e. starting at the above times each battery fires 2 rounds every ½ hour at alternative objectives.

A 88 & C 86 have 3 objectives and engage them in rotation.

The above night task lasts from 7.30 p.m. to 4.30 a.m.

A88

Bc AB 9am

L

516a 31

I9th DIVISIONAL ARTILLERY TIME TABLE.

(Bombardment)

4-30 a.m.	- 8 a.m.	Fire on parapets with H?E.
8 a.m.	- 2 p.m.	Howitzer bombardment on Selected spots.
2 p.m.	- 5-30 p.m.	Wire cutting. Observing stations.
5.30 p,m.	- 7-30 p.m.	Communication trenches.
7-30 p.m.	- 4-30 a.m.	2-gun salvos every $2\frac{1}{2}$ minutes; each Selected locality being engaged every half hour. Bursts of fire in conjunction with the Infantry on damaged parapets.

Counter Battery will work in conjunction with the Heavy Artillery.

I5/9/I5.

(Sd) C.C.Lawrie Brigadier General R.A.
Commanding I9th Division. R.A.

This is liable to alteration especially as regards wire cutting.

19th Division

88th Bde: R.F.A.

Vol 3

Oct. 15

Instructions regarding War Diaries and Intelligence Summaries are contained in F. S. Regs., Part II. and the Staff Manual respectively. Title Pages will be prepared in manuscript.

WAR DIARY
or
INTELLIGENCE SUMMARY
(Erase heading not required.)

Army Form C. 2118

Place	Date	Hour	Summary of Events and Information	Remarks and references to Appendices
	1/10/15		The day passed without noteworthy incident.	
X 17 d 9.7	2/10/15		This also was a quiet day. H.Q of the Brigade moved from the forward Report Centre to the former headquarters.	
	3/10/15	11 am	The morning was quiet on our front. The group was reconstituted being designated I and IV *	
		3 pm	B Battery 88 were shelled with 5.9" hows about eight in all. The last shell but one struck the dug-out in which Capt Chance, who was O.C, 2nd Lt Hebblethwaite and five NCOs and men had taken refuge. It passed through the roof and burst inside, instantly killing all the occupants. This shell contained gas and four men who were digging the bodies out were overcome one being removed to hospital. All the bodies were removed during the afternoon and interred in the burial ground on the Rue du Bois at X 17 d 5.4. Enemy's trench mortars very active opposite Ferme du Bois	
	4/10/15		Captain J.O. Campbell was posted from Adjutant to command B-88. * The Indian IV Arty. Group composes the four batteries of 88th Brigade, the 59th battery R.F.A less one section and D 89 (Hows). Their zone extends from the Ferme Cour d'Avoué on the south to a hundred yards north of the Boar's Head S 16 a 3.7. Lt A Beal took over the duties of Adjutant and 2/Lt [illegible] was attached from C-88 & A-88 vice Lt Beal. B-88 moved to a new position during night at S10 d 4.0. Lt G.V. Douglas was posted to B-88 from D.A.C. The day was quiet but during the night the enemy were very active	
		11 pm	About 11 pm their 77 mm batteries opened fire on the Rue de Bois and proceeded to search the neighbouring ground as far as the Rue des Charattes.	
	5/10/15	2 am	Fire became more rapid especially in the neighbourhood of the Boar's Head where there was considerable bombing and rifle fire.	

Instructions regarding War Diaries and Intelligence Summaries are contained in F. S. Regs., Part II. and the Staff Manual respectively. Title Pages will be prepared in manuscript.

WAR DIARY
or
INTELLIGENCE SUMMARY
(Erase heading not required.)

Army Form C. 2118

Place	Date	Hour	Summary of Events and Information	Remarks and references to Appendices
	12/10/15	12.30 –4 pm	Batteries fired a few rounds at intervals at request of infantry. 77mm guns searched about the Rue du Bois rather more than usual. 2/Lt T.R. Dixon was posted to the Brigade and attached to [illegible]	
	13/10/15	12.30 –2 pm	A feint attack took place. At 1.5 p	
		1.5 p	Smoke bombs were fired all along the [illegible]. The enemy's batteries at once opened fire at our front line and support [illegible] with their 77mm guns using both shrapnel and H.E. Our guns commencing firing in accordance with the accompanying programme a few seconds before the smoke commenced. The wind was blowing from S.S.W. and consequently part of our front line [illegible] the fair breeze carried the smoke in a [illegible] direction [illegible] at once became impossible. The enemy's [illegible] the whole time but the 77mm batteries continued their fire until our guns ceased. A few 10cm hows. fell near [illegible] on the Rue du Bois but no damage was done. [illegible] and a section of the 97th [illegible] the 59th batteries confined their attention [illegible] front line, support and communication trenches [illegible]. [illegible] of shrapnel were fired by the [illegible]. [illegible] placed for enfilade fire and lent to [illegible] D 58 fired 48 rounds on active hostile batteries. During the afternoon [illegible] a number of 15cm + 10cm shells were sent into [illegible] and Vieille Chapelle including some gas shells. The attack did not appear to deceive the enemy on this front but succeeded in drawing a fair amount of artillery fire in retaliation.	

1875 Wt. W593/826 1,000,000 4/15 J.B.C. & A. A.D.S.S./Forms/C. 2118.

Instructions regarding War Diaries and Intelligence Summaries are contained in F. S. Regs., Part II. and the Staff Manual respectively. Title Pages will be prepared in manuscript.

WAR DIARY
or
INTELLIGENCE SUMMARY
(Erase heading not required.)

Army Form C. 2118

Place	Date	Hour	Summary of Events and Information	Remarks and references to Appendices
	5/10/15	3.45 am	Heavy rifle fire was exchanged above the Boar's Head. Our batteries fired a few rounds and silenced the firing on our front. The remainder of day was normal.	
		5.45 pm	Peculiar lights, which appeared to be fire balloons burning about 3,000 ft up over the enemy's lines behind the Cour d'Avoué. They passed gradually towards the Ferme du Bois. Ten were observed in all by the F.O.O.s of C-88 & the 59th. Similar lights were seen at 8.45 by the O.C. D-89.	
	6/10/15	3.30 pm	Enemy's trench mortars were active at Boar's Head. D.88 retaliated on hostile batteries with required effect. B-88 having reconstructed their position began registration.	
	7/10/15	→	During the afternoon our batteries were active especially D-89 who took part in a small bombardment on the part of Indian III. D-89 fired 42 rounds with good effect on the enemy's front line parapet.	
	8/10/15	3.45 - 5.5 pm	D-88 fired 50 rounds at hostile batteries with the result that no action by hostile artillery was reported on the following day. A 10 cm How. fired 13 rounds on the Rue des Chavattes during the afternoon some rounds being near A-88.	
	9/10/15		Weather very misty. Quiet day. Cheering was heard in enemy front line opposite our front from 9.45 pm – 9.50 pm.	
	10/10/15		Batteries did some shooting, light being better. D.89 destroyed a machine gun cupola that enemy were rebuilding after a previous shelling. A-88 did some registration with aeroplane on two targets.	
	11/10/15		In the afternoon four batteries of the group retaliated for some activity on the part of enemy 77 mm and 10 cm batteries. 2 Hostile aeroplanes were seen from 3.15 – 4 pm reconnoitring our lines.	

1875 Wt. W593/826 1,000,000 4/15 J.B.C. & A. A.D.S.S./Forms/C. 2118.

Instructions regarding War Diaries and Intelligence Summaries are contained in F. S. Regs., Part II. and the Staff Manual respectively. Title Pages will be prepared in manuscript.

WAR DIARY
or
INTELLIGENCE SUMMARY
(Erase heading not required.)

Army Form C. 2118

Place	Date	Hour	Summary of Events and Information	Remarks and references to Appendices
	13/10/15	4.5 pm	B-88 registered 3 targets by ballon observation.	
		2.10 pm	The enemy fired a few French shells into [illegible] fuzes were picked up. They were apparently 6".	
	14/10/15	11.30 am	A large number of minenwerfer bombs were fired on our front [illegible] the Boar's Head. The 59th Batty and C-88 retaliated [illegible] on the trenches and trolley lines around the Ferme du Bois where [illegible] located. The bombing ceased at 12.30 pm. [illegible] C-88 retaliated on the enemy's trenches in S16d and S22a.	
	15/10/15		The day passed very quietly. Weather misty.	
	16/10/15	2-3.30 pm	A similar day. 77mm shells, about 15 in number [illegible] at S15a.	
	17/10/15		A very quiet day. Only 9 rounds fired by the Group. [illegible] difficult owing to haze.	
	18/10/15		Enemy's field guns active on the Rue du Bois during the morning. D 88 retaliated on well-known active batteries and A 88 & C 88 retaliated on hostile trenches.	
	19/10/15		During the morning all batteries fired 12 rounds each on various points in enemy's trenches as dictated by Col. [illegible] such as converging trolley lines & communication trenches etc. The enemy in return fired some 4.2 & 5.9 hows on our support trenches in neighbourhood of Embankment Trench.	
	20/10/15		All batteries again carried out a similar shoot to yesterday on different localities at various times during day.	

1875 Wt. W593/826 1,000,000 4/15 J.B.C. & A. A.D.S.S./Forms/C. 2118.

Army Form C. 2118

WAR DIARY
or
INTELLIGENCE SUMMARY
(Erase heading not required.)

Instructions regarding War Diaries and Intelligence Summaries are contained in F. S. Regs., Part II. and the Staff Manual respectively. Title Pages will be prepared in manuscript.

Place	Date	Hour	Summary of Events and Information	Remarks and references to Appendices
	20/10/15	3–5 pm	The enemy again retaliated with his field howitzer firing over 30, 4.2 shells on S15 a 2.5 without doing any damage.	
			D.89 destroyed a house used as an O.P at S17 a 5.9 at request of Meerut Divnl. Arty. 20 rounds were fired in all.	
	~~21/10/15~~		The Garhwal Infantry Brigade having taken over the front held by the 57th Infy Bde which this Arty Group was covering and the new zone being slightly more north, A 88 covered from S16 c 5.2 – Fme du Bois, C-88 from Fme du Bois – S16 a 6.6 and 59th Bty S16 a 6.6 – S10 c 8.1. The How. Battery relieving B 88 commenced to alter the gun pits so that the guns of B 88 remained on the battery position in reserve.	
	21/10/15	10 am.	I and IV became I and III Arty Group and came under the orders of the G.O.C. Meerut Divnl Arty.	
		5.45 pm + 7 pm	Enemy fired minenwerfer bombs at Door's Head but very prompt retaliation for C 88 + 59th Bty effectively stopped it. The day was quiet especially the morning.	
	22/10/15		Batteries fired some 60 rounds during the afternoon without eliciting much response from enemy. At night sections of A 88, D 88 & C 88 relieved as per accompanying orders	

1875 Wt. W593/826 1,000,000 4/15 J.B.C. & A. A.D.S.S./Forms/C. 2118.

Army Form C. 2118

Instructions regarding War Diaries and Intelligence Summaries are contained in F. S. Regs., Part II. and the Staff Manual respectively. Title Pages will be prepared in manuscript.

WAR DIARY
or
INTELLIGENCE SUMMARY
(Erase heading not required.)

Place	Date	Hour	Summary of Events and Information	Remarks and references to Appendices
	23/10/15		A quiet day. A 88 and C 88 dispersed working parties at 2.45 pm & 3.15 pm respectively in [illegible] and a communication trench. B 88 dispersed another in the same [illegible] at 8.30 pm. Enemy's artillery quiet. At night remaining sections of batteries withdrawn on relief. Batteries having been relieved remained at wagon lines in vicinity of canal near and west of [illegible]. D 88 remained in action as counter battery under new 2nd [illegible] group. Bde Amm Col + Headquarters also remained stationary.	
	24/10/15		Work commenced on forward position at (A-88) S 14 d 1.0 (B-88) S 14 d 3.1 and (C 88) S 20 b 3.5. Work carried on day and night.	
	25th 10/15		Work on forward positions continued.	
	26th 10/15 – 30th 10/15		do. (weather was continuously bad, rain falling intermittently)	
	31st 10/15		Forward positions completed and one gun of each battery registered.	

1875 Wt. W593/826 1,000,000 4/15 J.B.C. & A. A.D.S.S./Forms/C. 2118.

Copy No. 18.

Operation Order No. 95
by
Brigadier General C. G. Blackader, D.S.O.
Commanding Garhwal Brigade.

Reference maps:-
19th October 1915.

1/10000 36 S.W. Sheet 3.

1/40000 BETHUNE Sheet.

1. The Garhwal Brigade will take over the front held by the 57th Brigade from PIPE STREET exclusive to VINE STREET inclusive on the 20th October.
2. Reliefs in accordance with attached table. Details to be arranged between Commanding Officers concerned.
3. 2/8th Gurkhas will be relieved on front VINE STREET inclusive to CINDER TRACK inclusive by Dehra Dun Brigade on the 21st October and will be in Brigade Reserve.
4. All Posts and Keeps will be under the command of the Officer Commanding 3rd Londons. Minimum garrisons are as under:-

WATERS
FALLEN TREE
PALL MALL
DEAD COW
CHOCOLATE
CATS
FACTORY
HAYSTACK
PATH.
Z ORCHARD.
ALBERT
DOGS.
} 15 rifles each.

SCOTT
HUNTER
} a guard of 4 men each.

RICHEBOURG 30 rifles.

5. Stores will be taken over by daylight. Certificates of trench and post stores will be forwarded to Staff Captains by Sub Section Commanders and by

P.T.O.

by Officer Commanding, 3rd Londons for Posts.
6. Reports to LOISNE Chateau till 2 p.m. after that to White House, VIELLE CHAPELLE.

Major
Brigade Major, Garhwal Brigade.

Issued to Signals at 7.45 p.m.

Copy No 1. 2nd Leicesters
2. 3rd Londons.
3. 2/3rd Gurkhas
4. Garhwal Rifles
5. 2/8th Gurkhas
6. Bde Grenade Coy
7. Bde Bomb Gun Dett.
8. Bde Machine Gun Section.
9. No 5 Trench Mortar Battery
10 Bde. Signals.
11. 57th Brigade
12 Dehra Dun Brigade
13. Sirhind Brigade.
14. Meerut Division
15. C.R.A., Meerut Division
16. War Diary.
17. File
18. 88th Bde. R.F.A.

March Table accompanying Garhwal Brigade Operation Order No 95

Unit	To relieve	Guides to meet relieving Unit at.	Destination	Route	1st Line Depots at	Remarks.
2/3rd Gurkhas	10th Worcesters	C.M. CORNER 5-45 p.m.	PIPE STREET — FARM CORNER. (both exclusive).	LE TOURET — RUE DU BOIS	X. 4. b. 2. 7.	
Garhwal Rifles	8th Gloucesters	WINDY CORNER 5-45 p.m.	FARM CORNER (inclusive) — CINDER TRACK (exclusive.	Bridge X. 8. b. 4. 5 — Rd junction X. 4. d. — KING GEORGES Rd.	R. 34. c. 9. 2.	
2/8th Gurkhas	8th Gloucesters	WINDY CORNER 6 p.m.	CINDER TRACK - VINE STREET. (both inclusive).	Rd junction X. 10. d. — KING GEORGES ROAD.	X. 4. d. 5. 5.	
3rd Londons	10th Warwicks	—	Posts.	RUE DU BOIS	R. 34. d. 2. 3.	Reliefs to be complete by 2 p.m.
2nd Leicesters		—	Brigade Reserve ALBERT ROAD.	Follow Garhwal Rifles to EMPERORS' ROAD thence 2/8th Gurkhas	R. 34. d. 2. 3.	
Bde. Machine Guns.	Similar Unit	WINDY CORNER 9 a.m.	PIPE STREET — CINDER TRACK.	RUE DU BOIS — KINGS ROAD. — KING GEORGE'S ROAD.	KING GEORGE'S ROAD.	
Bde Bomb Gun Dett.	—	—	near BOARS' HEAD	Follow Garhwal Rifles	KING GEORGE'S ROAD.	
No 5 T. M. B.	—	—	— do —	— do —		
Bde Grenade Coy.	Similar Unit	—	RUE DES CHAVATTES.	As for Garhwal Rifles		Clear billets by 2 p.m.

Note 1. Billeting Officers to meet Staff Captain at WHITE HOUSE, VIE LLE CHAPELLE at 11 a.m. tomorrow.

Note 2. Depots will move at 2 p.m.

SECRET

IND II ARTILLERY GROUP.

Instructions for coming operations.

------ist.phase ; bombardment -------

------o-------

Group 1. The group consists of:-

(a) 4 wire cutting batteries B 88, C 88, C 86, D 86.

(b) 1 general duty battery A 88

(c) 1 counter battery D 88

(d) 1 H owitzer battery D 89

Bombardment.2. The preliminary bombardment is expected to last 4 days. Tasks , ammunition etc., allotted as per attached programme.

Tasks. 3. Tasks will be divided as follows:-

(a) Day --- ~~8~~ 4.30 a.m to ~~8~~ 7.30 p.m.

(b) Night-- 7.30 p.m. to 4.30.am.

(a) consists of wire cutting , enemy's first ~~and~~ second line and communication trenches. Observation Stations.

(b) shelling localities and preventing repair to wire.

Wire cutting 4. Batteries detailed for wire cutting will select a front of 50 yards in their own zones on which to cut wire -- approximately 12 yards per diem should be cut. The wire must be distinctly seen from O.ps. and Time shell with very low burst employed ---- a certain allotment of ammunition is made for nightfiring on points cut to prevent repair by the enemy. ~~The hour selected for wire cutting is left to battery commanders.~~

Night work. 5. Night tasks have been calculated to give an approximate allowance of 8 rounds per hour for 9 hours . Each 18 Pr. battery will be allotted 2 localities to shell at night and each locality will get 2 rounds every half hour.

List of battdries attached.

Counter batteries.

6. Counter batteries will work by day with the heavy artillery; by night will shell localities.

General duty battery.. 7. General duty battery will include in its tasks enfilade of roads and positions in IND. I. area.

Re-adjustment of front. 8. In the event of a re-adjustment of the IND II infantry front , the zones of the following batteries will be widened Southwards:- B 86 C 86 D 86.

Ammunition supply. 9. When authority is received and ammunition allotted, all battery and ammunition column echelons will be kept filled with ammunition ready for an immediate advance. Ammunition required for present operations will be dumped. Any of the dumped ammunition unexpended on an order to advance will be left behind on the position and collected by rear echelons such as D A C. etc.,

Return 10. Ammunition is not to be accumulated. A return of ammunition expended is to be sent in daily at 7 p.m.

Enemy trenches. 11. Batteries which shell trenches must pay special attention to enemy second line trenches on the 1st.and 2nd.

(3)

days and to the ~~second~~ first line trenches on the 3rd.& 4th.days

Allotment of localities.12. Localities are allotted as follows:-

A 88	S 27 d 3.6.	S 22 a 7.8.
B 88	S 22 c 8.6.	S 22 b 6.1.
C 88	RUE DE CAILLOUX and FERME DE BOIS	
D 88	FERME DE TOULOTTE and FERME COUR D'AVOUE.	
C 86	S 27 d 9.5.	S 28 d.3.1.
D 86	RUE DE MARAIS and cross roads in VIOLAINES.	
D 89	detailed separately	

---------O---------

Rokeby Lt Col
16/9/15

SECRET

TASKS AND AMMUNITION ALLOTTED TO BATTERIES OF IND. II GROUP.

....

A. Wire cutting batteries.

every day per battery.	S.	H.E.
(1) wure cutting (day)	60	
preventing repairs (night)	20	
(2) day tasks (1st & 2nd.line trenches.	48	56
(3) night tasks (localities)	32	40
Daily total	160	96

B. Counter battery.

every day per battery.	S.	H.E.
(1) counter work with heavy artillery.	120	56
(2) nighttasks (localities)	40	40
	160	96.

C. general duty battery.

	S.	H.E.
(1) ~~duty~~ day tasks 1st & 2nd.line trenches.	108	56
(2) night tasks. (localities)	52	40
	160	96

(2)

D. <u>Howitzer battery.</u>

	S.	H.E.
every day per battery	10	192.

~~Issues~~ Tasks detailed separately to O.C.

---

abk
16.9.15

MOVES OF WAGON LINES & AMMUNITION COLUMNS.

86th Brigade & D/88th Wagons will move into their new billets on 21st inst., being clear of their present billets by 10 a.m.

86th Bde. Ammunition Column will move into the billets now occupied by the 88th Bde. Ammunition Column on the 22nd inst., being clear of their present billets by 10 a.m.

87th Bde. Wagons will move into their new billets when their batteries come into action.

87th Bde. Ammunition Column move into their new billets on 22nd inst. ready to supply 87th Bde. by 10 a.m.

88th Bde. Ammunition Column (less section belonging to D/88th, which will come under orders of 86th Bde. Ammunition Column) will move into its new billets ~~by 10 a.m.~~ on 22nd being clear of present billets by 10 a.m.

89th Bde. Wagons & Ammunition Column will move into their new billets on the 21st inst., being clear of their present billets by 10 a.m.

19th October, 1915.

Captain, R.F.A.
Staff Captain, 19th Divl. Arty.

Copy No. 10......

19th Division Order No.13.

18th October 1915.

References to Corps Trench Map
and 1/40,000 combined sheet BETHUNE.

1. Meerut Division is handing over to 28th Division, 1st Corps, the front from the LA BASSEE Canal to THE LOOP (inclusive to 28th Divn), commencing on 19th inst. This relief to be completed by 6 a.m. 22nd inst.

Concurrently with this relief the front held by the Indian Corps will be readjusted as follows, commencing on 19th inst :-

<u>19th Divn</u>. from THE LOOP (exclusive) to CADBURY communication trench (exclusive). The new sections on this front will be numbered IND I and IND II.

<u>Meerut Divn</u>. thence to the LA BASSEE road exclusive.

<u>Lahore Divn</u>. thence to SUNKEN ROAD (exclusive).

2. The relief will be carried out in accordance with the attached March Table; details being arranged between Brigades or units concerned.

3. SHETLAND ROAD will belong to the new IND II, PIONEER ROAD to the new IND I; ARGYLE ROAD will be neutral. RICHMOND TRENCH will belong to the new IND II as far S. as its intersection with ARGYLE ROAD inclusive; RUE DE CAILLOUX, including CAILLOUX posts, will belong to IND II. Point of division on front line will be at junction of ORCHARD SUPPORT trench with S. side of Salient, inclusive to Ind II

4. Separate instructions will be issued regarding artillery reliefs and responsibility for posts.

5. No.11 TrenchMortar Battery, on transfer from Meerut Division on 20th, will be attached to 56th Bde, reporting at CSE. DU RAUX at 3-0 p.m.

6. Progress of reliefs will be reported to Divnl. H.Q.

7. G.Os.C. Bdes in front line will take over command of their new sections on completion of reliefs. Bde H.Q. will be - IND I -- LOISNE.
IND II -- CSE. DU RAUX.

8. Divisional H.Q. will close at FOSSE CHATEAU at 10 a.m. on 21st inst., and will open at LOCON at the same hour. At that hour G.O.C. 19th Divn. will assume command of the new Divnl. front.

Issued at 5-15 p.m.

A. E. Mullins [signature]
Lieutenant-Colonel,
General Staff.

Copies to :-
File.
War Diary.
G.O.C.
G.S.
A.A.&.Q.M.G.
G.O.C., R.A.
C.R.E.
56th Infy.Bde.
57th " "
58th " "
5/S.W.Borderers.
Divnl. Train.
M.M.Gun Battery.
A.D.M.S.
Indian Corps.
Lahore Division.
Meerut "
Divnl.Signal Coy.
" Cavalry.
" Cyclists.
28th Division.

MARCH TABLE --- 19TH DIVISION.

Date	Unit	From Area	Time	To Destination	Route	Remarks
October 20th	Portion of Battn. of 58th Bde. in Ind III(a).	ORKNEY Road(excl.) -- to junction of ORCHARD Support Trench and South side of Salient.	by 6-0 p.m.	As directed by G.O.C. 56th Bde.	PIONEER Road	Relieved by troops from one of the Reserve Bns. 57th Bde. To be arranged between Bdes.
20th	Portion of Bn. of 57th Bde. in Ind IV(a)	PIPE Commn. Trench -- to CADBURY (excl)	by 6-0 p.m.	Intermediate Line		To be relieved by 56th Bde. as arranged between Bdes.
20th	94th Fld.Coy.R.E.	COUR ST.VAAST	2-30 p.m.	Billets in X 10 c.	Bridge X 5 b 3.2. LACOUTURE -- LE TOURET road.	To be clear of its billets in COUR ST.VAAST by 2-30 p.m.
20th	57th Bde:- M.G.Coy. Grenadier Coy	Present billets		Vicinity of LOISNE.	Via LE TOURET.	Time to be arranged between 57th & Garhwal Bdes.
20th	5/S.W.B:- H.Qrs.& 1 Coy. 1 Coy. 1 Coy.	LE TOURET. " " " "		GORRE CHATEAU. Take over Posts from Dehra Dun Bde. Handle of TUNING FORK.		
20th	58th Bde.	PARADIS area and VIEILLE CHAPELLE.		LOCON area.	Via LES LOBES.	Not to arrive in new area before 4-0 p.m.
20th.	Divnl.Squadron.	LE QUENTIN.		LA PANNERIE.		

Date	Unit	From Area	Time	To Destination	Route	Remarks
October Night 20th/21st	1 Bn. 57th Bde.	Trenches) CADBURY to VINE STREET.		Intermediate line by ESTAMINET CORNER.	RUE DE L'EPINETTE	In support of new Ind I. — Relieved by Garhwal Bde.
	1 Bn. 57th Bde.	Trenches)		LACOUTURE (exclusive of farm at X 5 c 8.3.)		In support of new Ind III for the night. — Relieved by Garhwal Bde.
	2 Bns. 57th Bde.	Bde.Reserve.		Trenches from THE LOOP (exclusive) to ORKNEY Road (inclusive)		Relieving a portion of Dehra Dun Bde. Times etc. to be arranged between Bdes.
	H.Qrs. 57th Bde.	Present billets.	On complet-ion of relief.	LOISNE CHATEAU.		
21st	H.Qrs. 19th Divn.	FOSSE		LOCON		
	Divl.Cyclist Coy.	FOSSE.		W 11 b 2.8.		
	Divl.Sig.Sec.	"		Factory, LOCON.		
	Divl.Mob.Vet.Sec.	"		LOCON.		
21st	1 Bn. 57th Bde.	LACOUTURE		LE HAMEL.	Via LE TOURET.	Time to be arranged with Dehra Dun Bde.

N.B. The Battalion of 57th Brigade now garrisoning Posts and Keeps will be relieved as regards these garrisons by a Company from the Garhwal Brigade during afternoon of 20th instant. Orders as to Divl. Train and Field Ambulances will be issued later.

Copy No. 10.....

19th Division Order No.14.

19th October 1915.

Reference to 1/40,000 Combined Sheet ~~BETHUNE and Corps~~ Trench Map.

1. Meerut Division is handing over to 28th Division, 1st Corps, the front from the LA BASSEE Canal to GRENADIER ROAD (exclusive to 28th Divn); instead of as stated in 19th Division Order No.13 of yesterday, which is now cancelled.
The readjustment of the front held by the Indian Corps, mentioned in the above Operation Order, is therefore altered, and the 19th Division front will extend from junction of GRENADIER ROAD with the front line, at A 3 c 1.2., to PIPE Communication Trench, inclusive. The new sections on this front will be numbered IND I and IND II.

2. The relief will be carried out in accordance with the attached March Table; details being arranged between Brigades or units concerned.

3. The New Ind I section will extend from A 3 c 1.2 to ORKNEY ROAD (inclusive).
The present Ind III Section becomes the new Ind II, except that PIPE Communication Trench will be inclusive to it, instead of exclusive as at present.

4. Instructions with regard to artillery reliefs and responsibilit for posts are being issued separately.

5. No.11 Trench Mortar Battery, on transfer from Meerut Division on 20th, will be attached to 56th Bde in the new Ind II, reporting at CSE. DU RAUX at 3 p.m.

6. Progress of reliefs will be reported to Divnl. H.Q.

7. G.Os.C Bdes in front line will take over command of their new sections on completion of reliefs.
Bde. H.Q. will be Ind I --- LOISNE.
Ind II=== CSE. DU RAUX.

8. Divl. H.Q. will close at FOSSE CHATEAU at 10 a.m. on 21st inst and will open at LOCON at the same hour.
At that hour G.OC. 19th Division will assume command of the new Divisional Front.

Issued at 6.0 pm.

A. Buckle
Lieutenant-Colonel,
General Staff.

Copies to :-

File.	Divnl.Train.
War Diary.	M.M.Gun Battery.
G.O.C.	A.D.M.S.
G.S.	Indian Corps.
A.A &.Q.M.G.	Lahore Division.
G.O.C., R.A.	Meerut "
C.R.E.	Divnl.Signal Coy.
56th Infy.Bde.	" Cavalry.
57th " "	" Cyclists.
58th " "	28th Division.
5/S.W.Borderers.	7th Division.

MARCH TABLE --- 19TH DIVISION.

Date.	Unit.	From Area.	Time.	To destination.	Route.	Remarks.
October 20th.	94th Fld.Coy.R.E.	COUR ST.VAAST	2-30 p.m.	Billets in X 10 c.	Bridge X 5 b 3.2.LACOUTURE -- LE TOURET road.	To be clear of its billets in COUR ST. VAAST by 2-30 p.m.
20th.	57th Bde:- M.G.Coy. Grenadier Coy	Present billets		Vicinity of LOISNE	Via LE TOURET	Time to be arranged between 57th & Garhwal Bdes.
20th.	5/S.W.B:- H.Qrs.& 1 Coy. 1 Coy. 1 Coy.	LE TOURET. " "		GORRE CHATEAU. Take over posts from Dehra Dun Bde. Handle of TUNING FORK.		
20th.	58th Bde.	PARADIS area and VIEILLE CHAPELLE.		LOCON area.	Via LES LOBES.	Not to arrive in new area before 4-0 p.m.
20th.	Divl.Squadron.	LE QUENTIN.		LA PANNERIE.		
Night 20/21st.	1 Bn.57th Bde.	Trenches)PIPE Communication trench to VINE STREET.		Intermediate line by ESTAMINET CORNER.	RUE DE L'EPINETTE.	Relieved by Garhwal Bde.
	1 Bn.57th Bde.	Trenches		LE HAMEL.	RUE DU BOIS.	
	2 Bns.57th Bde.	Bde.Reserve.		Trenches from GRENADIER RD (incl) to ORKNEY Road (inclusive).		Relieving Dehra Dun Bde. Times etc. to be arranged between Bdes.
	H.Qrs.57th Bde.	Present billets.	On completion of relief.	LOISNE.		
21st.	H.Qrs.19th Divn. Divl.Cyclist Coy Divl.San.Sec. Divnl.Mob.Vet.Sec	FOSSE. " " "		LOCON. W 11 b 2.8. Factory, LOCON. LOCON.		

N.B. The Battalion of 57th Brigade now garrisoning Posts and Keeps will be relieved as regards these garrisons by a Company from the Garhwal Brigade during afternoon of 20th instant.

S E C R E T. Copy No ...6...

INSTRUCTIONS FOR RELIEF.

No 8.

XIXth DIVISIONAL ARTILLERY.

19th Divisional Artillery Instructions No 7 are cancelled and the following substituted.

1. The 19th Divisional Artillery on readjustment of the line being completed will support the front from the junction of GRENADIER ROAD with front line trench at A.3.c.1.2. to PIPE Communication Trench inclusive. The command of the Artillery supporting this front will be taken over by the G.O.C. 19th Divisional Artillery at 10am 21st October, after which reports will be sent to LOGON.

2. At 10 a.m. 21st October 88th F.A.Brigade, less "D" Battery comes under orders of MEERUT Divisional Artillery. "D" Battery 88th F.A.Brigade and "D" Battery 89th F.A.Brigade come under the orders of O.C. 86th F.A. Brigade.

3. At the above hour IND.I. Artillery Group will take over support of the line from A.3.c.1.2. to ORKNEY ROAD inclusive. IND.II. Artillery Group will support the line thence to PIPE Communication Trench inclusive.

4. The composition of Artillery Groups from 10 a.m. 21st October will be as follows:-

IND. I. Artillery Group.

Group Commander - Lieut.-Colonel J.A. Tyler.
H.Qrs. at X.22.d.3.2.
2nd Battery R.F.A.
8th Battery R.F.A.
14th Battery R.F.A.
44th Battery R.F.A.
"A"/89th F.A.Brigade.

IND.II. Artillery Group.

Group Commander - Lieut.-Colonel A.E.Wilson.
H.Qrs. at X.16.d.9.9.
86th F.A.Brigade.
"D"/88th F.A.Brigade. (Counter Battery)
"D"/89th F.A.Brigade.

5. On the night 21st/22nd inst., Sections of the 2nd, 8th, 14th and 44th Batteries R.F.A. 13th F.A.Brigade, will be relievdd by Sections of the 87th F.A.Brigade.

6. At 10 a.m., 22nd inst., Brigade and Battery Commanders 87th F.A.Brigade will assume Command of composite Batteries, IND.I. Artillery Group.

7. During the 22nd inst., Ammunition Column 87th F.A. Brigade will take over supply of Ammunition to the Infantry Brigade and Batteries holding IND.I.

8. Night 22nd/23rd inst. remaining Sections 13th F.A.Brigade will be relieved by Sections 87th F.A. Brigade.

9. 88th F.A.Brigade (less "D" Battery) will be relieved during the nights 23rd/24th and 24th/25th insts. by 4th F.A.Brigade.

10. Times and details of all reliefs will be arranged between Brigade Commanders concerned.

Major R.F.A.

20th October 1915. Brigade Major R.A. 19th Division.

Issued at 4.45pm.

Copies To:-

War Diary.
File.
B.G.R.A., Indian Corps.
19th Division.
IND.III. Artillery Group.
IND.IV. Artillery Group.
87th F.A.Brigade.
89th F.A.Brigade.
19th Divl. Ammn. Column.
LAHORE Divl. Artillery.
13th F.A.Brigade.
MEERUT Divl. Artillery.
28th Divl. Artillery.
17th Brigade R.G.A.
6th Kite and Balloon Section.
10th Squadron R.F.A.
56th Infantry Brigade.
57th Infantry Brigade.
58th Infantry Brigade.

----

16 (1)

SECRET. Copy No.....

MEERUT DIVISIONAL ARTILLERY OPERATION ORDER No.21.

Reference:- Map BETHUNE Combined Sheet 1/40,000 and Trench Map 1/10,000. 19th October 1915.

****

INTENTION. 1. MEERUT Division will hand over to 28th Division, 1st Corps the front from the LA BASSEE CANAL to GRENADIER ROAD exclusive, and, to the 57th Brigade, 19th Division, thence to ORKNEY ROAD (inclusive).

INDIAN CORPS' front will be readjusted as follows:-

<u>19th DIVISION</u>. From GRENADIER ROAD (inclusive) to PIPE Trench (inclusive);

<u>MEERUT DIVISION</u>. Thence to CRESCENT Trench (exclusive);

<u>LAHORE DIVISION</u>. Thence to SUNKEN ROAD (exclusive).

GARHWAL Brigade (and 1st Seaforths) will hand over their present front to 85th Brigade, 28th Division, on 19th instant.

DEHRA DUN Brigade (less 1st Seaforths) will hand over its present front GRENADIER ROAD (inclusive) to ORKNEY ROAD (inclusive) to 57th Brigade, 19th Division, on night of 20th/21st October.

The 85th Brigade will be relieved by an Infantry Brigade of 7th Division on 20th October.

ARTILLERY. 2. (a) Present IND.I. Artillery Group will remain on in support of 85th Brigade (28th Division) front CANAL to GRENADIER ROAD, and on its relief in support of a Brigade of the 7th Division.
It will be relieved itself by 7th Divisional Artillery under instructions to issue later. At 10.a.m. on 21st October it will come under the orders of 7th Division. (?)

(b) IND.II. Artillery Group will become IND.I. Artillery Group at 10.a.m. on 21st October, when it will come under the orders of G.O.C., R.A., 19th Division.
The batteries of this Group will be relieved by 87th Brigade R.F.A. under orders to issue later.

(c) At 10.a.m. on 21st October 88th Brigade less "D" Battery (19th Divisional Artillery) comes under the orders of G.O.C., R.A., MEERUT Division, and will be responsible for the support of the GARHWAL Brigade on the front "PIPE" to CINDER TRACK.
O.C. Lt Colonel A.D. KIRBY, R.F.A. Hd Qrs X 17 d 7'8.

(d) On night 21st/22nd October on relief of SIRHIND Brigade by DEHRA DUN Brigade, 93rd, 94th and 1 Section of 59th Batteries, also C/89 Howitzer Battery will come under the orders of G.O.C., R.A., MEERUT Division.
Artillery Group Commander-Lt Colonel R.G. OUSELEY, C.M.G., D.S.O., R.F.A. Hd Qrs R 29 c.d.

(e) Details of reliefs of 4th, 9th and 13th Brigades R.F.A. will issue later.

AMMUNITION SUPPLY. 3. <u>During the 22nd October</u>-4th Brigade R.F.A. Ammunition Column takes over the supply of ammunition to the Infantry Brigade holding front IND. III.;
87th Brigade R.F.A. Ammunition Column takes over supply of ammunition to the Infantry Brigade holding front IND.I.; and
13th Brigade R.F.A. Ammunition Column takes over supply of ammunition to Infantry Brigade on front IND.IV.;
9th Brigade R.F.A. Ammunition Column taking over supply of S.A.A. to BAREILLY Brigade.

P.T.O.

REPORTS & COMMAND. 4. MEERUT Divisional Artillery Headquarters will close at LOCON and open at the CHATEAU at CROIX MARMEUSE at 10.a.m. on 21st October, at which time the G.O.C., MEERUT Division assumes command of the new front.

R. K. Lynch-Staunton.

Major R.A.

Brigade Major, Royal Artillery,
MEERUT DIVISION.

Issued at 9.30.p.m. by motor cyclist to:-

Copy No. 1 to MEERUT DIVISION.
,, 2 to 7th DIVISION.
,, 3 to Brigadier General R.A., INDIAN CORPS.
,, 4 to 2nd Divisional Artillery.
,, 5 to 7th Divisional Artillery.
,, 6 to 19th Divisional Artillery.
,, 7 to LAHORE Divisional Artillery.
,, 8 to BAREILLY Brigade.
,, 9 to GARHWAL Brigade.
,, 10 to DEHRA DUN Brigade.
,, 11 to 85th Brigade(28th Division).
,, 12 to 4th Brigade R.F.A.
,, 13 to 9th Brigade R.F.A.
,, 14 to 13th Brigade R.F.A.
,, 15 to 131st Howitzer Brigade R.F.A.
,, 16 to 88th Brigade R.F.A.(19th Divisional Artillery).
,, 17 to 18th Brigade R.F.A.(LAHORE Divisional Artillery).
,, 18 to 17th Brigade R.G.A.
,, 19 to MEERUT Divisional Ammunition Column.
,, 20 War Diary.
,, 21 File.

S E C R E T . Copy No. 12 (2)

I N S T R U C T I O N S

MEERUT DIVISIONAL ARTILLERY.

Reference-MEERUT DIVISIONAL ARTILLERY OPERATION ORDER No.21 dated the 19th October 1915, the following additions are notified:-

INFANTRY RELIEFS.

1. GARHWAL Brigade will take over the front held by the 57th Brigade from PIPE STREET(exclusive) to VINE STREET(inclusive) on 20th October.

2. 2nd/8th Gurkhas(GARHWAL Brigade) will be relieved on the front VINE STREET to CINDER TRACK, both inclusive, by DEHRA DUN Brigade on 21st October.

3. DEHRA DUN Brigade will take over front CINDER TRACK(inclusive) to CRESCENT COMMUNICATION TRENCH(exclusive) on night 21st/22nd October.

ARTILLERY.

The Artillery support of the GARHWAL Brigade will now be as follows, and not as laid down in my No.1385-R.A.(L) dated 19th October 1915:-

GARHWAL BRIGADE FRONT:- IND. III. ARTILLERY GROUP.

Group Commander........................Lt Colonel A.D. KIRBY, R.F.A.

Headquarters at..............................X 17 d 7'8.

Battery	Position	Guns
A/88 Battery R.F.A.	S 7 d 6'5	4 guns.
B/88 Battery R.F.A.	S 7 b 2'9	4 guns.
C/88 Battery R.F.A.	S 7 b 2'6	4 guns.
also		
59th Battery R.F.A. (LAHORE D.A.)	S 1 d 4'8	4 guns.

~~while GARHWAL Brigade covers frontage CINDER TRACK to VINE STREET, after which it joins IND. IV. Artillery Group.~~
This Group comes under the orders of G.O.C., R.A., MEERUT Division at 10.a.m. on 21st October 1915.
The O.C. this Group has a call on a 4'5 How Btty of 19th D.A. in case of attack.

DEHRA DUN BRIGADE FRONT. IND. IV. ARTILLERY GROUP.

Group Commander...................Lt Colonel R.G. OUSELEY, C.M.G.,D.S.O. R.F.A.

Headquarters at..............................R 29 c.d.

Battery	Position	Guns
94th Battery R.F.A.	M 31 d 8'7	5 guns.
	S 14 a 7'5	1 gun.
93rd Battery R.F.A.	M 32 a 3'6	4 guns.
	M 34 c 2'8	2 guns.
59th Battery R.F.A.	S 14 a 4'5	2 guns for enfilade.
C/89 Howitzer Battery	M 32 b 5'5.	

~~This Group will be reinforced by 4 guns of *59th Battery R.F.A. at S 1 d 4'7 at the time DEHRA DUN Brigade takes over frontage CINDER TRACK to VINE STREET.~~ (*From IND. III. Artillery Group)

The G.O.C., R.A., MEERUT Division assumes command of this Group from G.O.C., R.A., LAHORE Division, at time that SIRHIND Brigade hands over command to DEHRA DUN Brigade.

ARTILLERY RELIEFS.

The relief of the MEERUT Division Batteries by the 7th, 19th and LAHORE Division Batteries will be arranged later.

P.T.O.

REPORTS.

The Headquarters, MEERUT Divisional Artillery will close at LOCON and open at the CHATEAU at CROIX MARMEUSE at 10.a.m. on 21st October.

Major R.A.

Brigade Major, Royal Artillery,
MEERUT DIVISION.

Issued at 12 noon.to:-

Copy No. 1 to MEERUT Division.
,, 2 to Brigadier General R.A., INDIAN Corps.
,, 3 to 19th Divisional Artillery.
,, 4 to LAHORE Divisional Artillery.
,, 5 to BAREILLY Brigade.
,, 6 to GARHWAL Brigade.
,, 7 to DEHRA DUN Brigade.
,, 8 to 4th Brigade R.F.A.
,, 9 to 9th Brigade R.F.A.
,, 10 to 13th Brigade R.F.A.
,, 11 to 131st Howitzer Brigade R.F.A.
,, 12 to 88th Brigade R.F.A.(19th D.A.)
,, 13 to 18th Brigade R.F.A.(LAHORE D.A.)
,, 14 to 17th Brigade R.G.A.
,, 15 to MEERUT Divisional Ammunition Column.
,, 16 to War Diary.
,, 17 to File.

S E C R E T . Copy No..15....

(3)

INSTRUCTIONS FOR RELIEF
of
BATTERIES OF MEERUT DIVISIONAL ARTILLERY.

In continuation of "INSTRUCTIONS MEERUT DIVISIONAL ARTILLERY" of to-days date, the following re-grouping and reliefs will take place:-

G R O U P I N G.

1. At 10.a.m. on 21st October Major A.D. MUSGRAVE, R.F.A. Commanding present IND. I. Artillery Group will become local C.R.A. for 7th Division. Headquarters 7th Division will run a line to his Headquarters by 10.a.m.
2. At 10.a.m. on 21st October, 2nd Battery R.F.A. again comes under control of IND. II. Artillery Group.
3. At 10.a.m. on 21st October, present IND. II. Artillery Group, (reinforced as in 2 above) will come under the direct command of the G.O.C., R.A., 19th Division, and will be known as IND. I.

R E L I E F S .

NIGHT of 21st/22nd:-

1 Section of a 7th Division Battery will relieve 1 Section B/87 Battery.
1 Section of each of 87th Brigade Batteries will relieve 2 Sections each of 2nd, 8th, 44th and 14th Batteries, which will withdraw to their wagon lines on relief.

NIGHT of 22nd/23rd:-

1 Section of a 7th Division Battery will relieve 1 Section B/87 Battery.
1 Section of each of 87th Brigade Batteries will relieve 1 Section each of 2nd, 8th, 44th and 14th Batteries, which will withdraw to their wagon lines on relief.
2 Sections(1 frontal and 1 enfilade) of 59th Battery will be relieved by 1 Section of 14th Battery()frontal) and 1 Section of 44th Battery(enfilade).
2 Sections(1 frontal and 1 detached) 93rd Battery will be relieved by 1 Section of 2nd Battery(frontal) and 1 Section of 14th Battery (detached).
1 gun of 94th Battery will be relieved by 1 gun of 8th Battery(enfilade), and 2 guns of 94th Battery will be relieved by 2 guns of 8th Battery(frontal).

NIGHT of 23rd/24th:-

1 Section 59th Battery will be relieved by 1 Section 14th Btty)
1 Section 93rd Battery will be relieved by 1 Section 2nd Btty)Frontal.
3 guns 94th Battery will be relieved by 3 guns of 8th Battery)
7th Divisional Artillery Batteries relieve Sections of 19th, 20th and 28th Batteries, which proceed to Rest Billets; and of 7th, 66th and 61st(How:)Batteries, which relieve sections of 88th Brigade Batteries forthwith.

NIGHT of 24th/25th:-

7th Divisional Artillery Batteries complete relief of 19th, 20th and 28th Batteries, which proceed to Rest Billets; and of 7th, 66th and 61st(How) Batteries, which complete relief of 88th Brigade Batteries forthwith.

C O M M A N D .

At 10.a.m. on 22nd October Brigade and Battery Commanders 87th Brigade R.F.A. assume command of composite batteries of the new IND. I. Artillery Group from MEERUT Divisional Artillery. Batteries

P.T.O.

COMMAND(continued)

At 10a.m. on 23rd October Brigade and Battery Commanders of new IND. IV. Artillery Group assume command from LAHORE Divisional Artillery.

Command of 7th Divisional Artillery Group(CANAL-ORKNEY ROAD) and of new IND. III. Artillery Group will be arranged later.

Times and details of all reliefs will be arranged between Artillery Brigade Commanders concerned.

R.K. Lynch-Staunton

Major R.A.

No.1390-R.A.(L).

Brigade Major, Royal Artillery,
MEERUT DIVISION.

20th October 1915.

Issued at 4.p.m. to:-

Copy No. 1 to MEERUT Division.
,, 2 to 7th Division.
,, 3 to Brigadier General R.A., INDIAN CORPS.
,, 4 to 2nd Divisional Artillery.
,, 5 to 7th Divisional Artillery.
,, ~~6 to 19th Divisional Artillery.~~
,, 7 to LAHORE Divisional Artillery.
,, 8 to BAREILLY Brigade.
,, 9 to GARHWAL Brigade.
,, 10 to DEHRA DUN Brigade.
,, 11 to 4th Brigade R.F.A.
,, 12 to 9th Brigade R.F.A.
,, 13 to 13th Brigade R.F.A.
,, 14 to 131st Howitzer Brigade R.F.A.
,, 15 to 88th Brigade R.F.A.(19th D.A.)
,, 16 to 18th Brigade R.F.A.(LAHORE D.A.)
,, 17 to 87th Brigade R.F.A.(19th D.A)
,, 18 to MEERUT Divisional Ammunition Column.
,, 19 to WAR DIARY.
,, 20 to FILE.

(4)

No.1396-R.A.(L).

Headquarters Divisional Artillery,
MEERUT DIVISION.

S E C R E T .

21st October 1915.

To,
The Headquarters,
88th Brigade R.F.A. ✓

Reference the attached, the 4 guns of 59th Battery (not the enfilade section in S 14 a) will remain attached to IND. III. Artillery Group under your command and will be available to cover from CINDER TRACK to S 16 a 1½'5.

Will you kindly arrange during the course of to-day and tomorrow for the following registration to be carried out:-

C/88 Battery, frontage S 16 a 1½'5 to FARM CORNER.

A/88 Battery, frontage FARM CORNER to PIPE TRENCH.

The reason that this is necessary is that during pending reliefs, the present position of B/88 will be being converted to a Howitzer position(for 61st Howitzer Battery) and the services of this battery will be lost. The C/88(7th) and A/88(66th) will therefore be required to cover this frontage during the relief.

Please note that the ~~XXXX~~ 7th Battery will be putting one Section into action to-night alongside the two Sections of C/88 Battery.

O.C. C/88 Battery might kindly have this Section registered tomorrow.

Also if possible the 14th Battery will put an enfilade Section into action at PONT LOGY to-night.

R. K. Lynch-Staunton.

Major R.A.

Brigade Major, Royal Artillery,
MEERUT DIVISION.

Copy to O.C. 4th Bde R.F.A for information.

(5)

SECRET.

No.1395-R.A.(L).

Headquarters, Divisional Artillery,
MEERUT DIVISION.

21st October 1915.

MEMORANDUM.

Reference SECRET "INSTRUCTIONS MEERUT DIVISIONAL ARTILLERY" dated the 20th October 1915.

Under Heading ARTILLERY:-

GARHWAL BRIGADE FRONT:-

After "59th Battery R.F.A.......S 1 d 4'8........4 guns" delete from "While GARHWAL Brigade" to "joins IND. IV. Artillery Group".

DEHRA DUN Brigade FRONT:-

Delete from "This Group will be reinforced" to "to VINE STREET".

NOTE:- 4 guns 59th Battery will remain attached to IND. III. Artillery Group, and the enfilade Section 59th Battery will remain attached to IND. IV. Artillery Group. The adjustment of the line from CINDER TRACK to VINE STREET will not alter the grouping of this battery.

R. K. Lynch-Staunton
Major R.A.

Brigade Major, Royal Artillery,
MEERUT DIVISION.

Copies issued to:-

MEERUT Division.
Brigadier General R.A., INDIAN CORPS.
LAHORE Divisional Artillery.
BAREILLY Brigade.
GARHWAL Brigade.
DEHRA DUN Brigade.
4th Brigade R.F.A.
13th Brigade R.F.A.
88th Brigade R.F.A.(19th D.A.)
18th Brigade R.F.A.(LAHORE D.A.)

SECRET.

BRIGADE ORDERS
by Lieut: Col: A.D.Kirby,R.F.A.
Commanding IND. IV.

Reliefs: Extracts from R.A. & Divnl: Orders.

1. Meerut Division is handing over to 28th Division, Ist Corps, the front from the LA BASSEE Canal to THE LOOP (inclusive to 28th Divn:), commencing on 19th inst.
This relief to be completed by 6 a.m. 22nd inst.
Concurrently with this relief the front held by the Indian Corps will be readjusted as follows, commencing on 19th inst:-

19th Divn:	from THE LOOP (exclusive) to CADBURY communication trench (exclusive). The new sections on this front will be numbered IND I. and IND II.
Meerut Divn:	thence to the LA BASSEE road exclusive.
Lahore Divn:	thence to SUNKEN ROAD (exclusive).

2. Divisional H.Q. will close at FOSSE CHATEAU at 10 a.m. on 21st inst., and will open at LOCON at the same hour.
At that hour G.O.C. 19th Divn: will assume command of the new Divnl: front.

3. At 10 a.m., 21st October, 88th F.A.Brigade, less "D" Battery comes under orders of MEERUT Divisional Artillery. "D" Battery 88th F.A. Brigade, and "D" Battery 89th F.A. Brigade come under orders of O.C. 86th F.A.Brigade.

4. IND II. Artillery Group will consist of 86th F.A.Brigade, "D" Battery 88th Brigade (Counter Battery), and "D" Battery 89th F.A.Brigade.

5. On the night 23rd/24th insts., Sections 4th F.A.Brigade will relieve Sections "A" "B" and "C" Batteries 88th F.A.Brigade and of 59th Battery R.F.A.

6. At 3 p.m. 24th October, Brigade and Battery Commanders 4th F.A. Brigade assume Command of composite Batteries 4th and 88th F.A. Brigades.

7. During the 24th October, Ammunition Column 4th F.A. Brigade takes over the supply of ammunition to the Infantry Brigade and Batteries holding IND III. (at present IND IV.)

8. Night 24th/25th inst. remaining Sections 4th F.A.Brigade will relieve remaining Sections 88th F.A.Brigade.

19. On relief, the 88th F.A.Brigade will proceed to rest billets at RUE DES VACHES.

9. On relief, the 88th Brigade Ammunition Column will supply ammunition to the Infantry Brigade in Reserve.

II. Times and details of all reliefs will be arranged between Brigade Commanders concerned.

I2. "D"/88 Wagons will move into their new billets on 24th inst., being clear of their present billets by 10 a.m.

I3. 86th Brigade Ammunition Column will move into the billets now occupied by the 88th Brigade Ammunition Column when "A" "B" and "C" Batteries 88th Brigade have moved into reserve.
The date will be notified in operation orders.

I4. 88th Brigade Ammunition Column (less section belonging to D/88, which will come under orders of 86th Brigade Amm: Column) will move into its new billets ~~[illegible]~~ as specified in para I3 hereof.

I5. The Garhwal Infantry Brigade will take over the front held by the 57th Brigade from PIPE STREET exclusive to VINE STREET inclusive on the 20th October.
All Posts and Keeps will be under the Command of the Officer Commanding 3rd Londons.

I6. The 2/3rd Gurkhas will relieve I0th Worcesters and the Garhwal Rifles, and 2/8th Gurkhas will relieve the 5th Gloucesters.
The 2/3rd Gurkhas will hold from PIPE STREET to FARM CORNER.

The Garhwal Rifles will hold from FARM CORNER to CINDER TRACK.

The 2/8th Gurkhas will hold from CINDER TRACK to VINE STREET.

Lieut: R.F.A.
Adjutant IND IV.

20/ I0/I5.

19th Dn

Nov 1915

88th Bde: R.F.A.

Vol: 4

121/7928

Instructions regarding War Diaries and Intelligence Summaries are contained in F. S. Regs., Part II. and the Staff Manual respectively. Title Pages will be prepared in manuscript.

WAR DIARY
or
INTELLIGENCE SUMMARY
(Erase heading not required.)

Army Form C. 2118

Place	Date	Hour	Summary of Events and Information	Remarks and references to Appendices
Rue du Bois X17d 8.8	1/11/15		Still in reserve. Work on forward positions completed. Ground very wet.	
P29 b 5.5	2/11/15		Marched to rest billets at RODECQ and neighbourhood. D 88 and its section of Bde Amm. Col remained in action in their present positions. A, B and C batteries and the other three sections of the Bde Amm. Col commenced cleaning up and taking down guns and thoroughly overhauling them. Col. A.D. Kirby returned to England on promotion.	
	3/11/15		Resting.	
	4/11/15		do.	
	5/11/15		do.	
	6/11/15		do.	
	7/11/15		do.	
	8/11/15		do.	
	9/11/15		3 guns of A-88 went into action at S7 d 8.3 (2 guns) and M34 a 5.3 (enfilade gun) taking over from 66th Battery RFA; B-88 went into action in an unoccupied position at S8 a 7.9; 3 guns C-88 went into action at S7 b 2.8 relieving a section of 7th Battery RFA; 3 sections of Bde Amm. Col returned to their former position at R32 d 3.7. Reliefs were effected at 5 pm. Major G.S. Tovey took over command of 88th Brigade.	46th Divl Arty Operation Order No 25 5/11/15 Meerut Divl Arty Instructions — 19th Divl Arty Operation Order 129 7/11/15

1875 Wt. W593/826 1,000,000 4/15 J.B.C. & A. A.D.S.S./Forms/C. 2118.

Army Form C. 2118

Instructions regarding War Diaries and Intelligence Summaries are contained in F. S. Regs., Part II. and the Staff Manual respectively. Title Pages will be prepared in manuscript.

WAR DIARY
or
INTELLIGENCE SUMMARY
(Erase heading not required.)

Place	Date	Hour	Summary of Events and Information	Remarks and references to Appendices
LA COUTURE X4 b 6.7	10/11/15	10am	Bde HQ moved up and took over command of Right Group of 46th Division from 4th F.A. Brigade. The Group consisted of A, B & C batteries 88th Bde, C-89 (Hows) at S1d 4.1 and 1st Battery Staffordshire R.F.A. at S1d 4.9. The zone of the Group extended from S16 a 3.7 to S22 a 3.4, C-89 also placed a gun at M34 c 4.0 to enfilade the whole front of this zone. The day was spent in registration. Weather dull and misty.	
		5pm	Remainder of reliefs effected.	
	11/10/15		Registration continued. Enemy's 5.9" hows fairly active on roads (Rue des Chavattes etc). Observation difficult owing to mist.	
	12/10/15		From 11am to 3pm the weather conditions were good for observation & taken advantage of by both sides. 66 5.9" hows (15% being blind) were fired at our O.P.s on Rue du Bois and House at corner of Albert Road absolutely demolished. The Nook was also hit 3 times but not much damaged. Enemies field guns were active throughout day on Rue du Bois. Our batteries retaliated heavily on Fme du Bois and support trenches along the front. 3 Enemy aeroplanes were seen from 7am to 10am.	
	13/10/15		1st Staffs Battery went under command of Centre Group 46th Divn. Our zone now extended from S16 a 5.1 to S22 a 3.4. C/89 however covered whole of former zone. Owing to the wet state of the enemy's trenches small parties of the enemy repeatedly exposed themselves during the afternoon. They were dispersed whenever they offered a good target by D-88. Otherwise a quiet day.	

1875 Wt. W593/826 1,000,000 4/15 J.B.C. & A. A.D.S.S./Forms/C. 2118.

Army Form C. 2118

Instructions regarding War Diaries and Intelligence Summaries are contained in F. S. Regs., Part II. and the Staff Manual respectively. Title Pages will be prepared in manuscript.

WAR DIARY
or
INTELLIGENCE SUMMARY
(Erase heading not required.)

Place	Date	Hour	Summary of Events and Information	Remarks and references to Appendices
	14/11/15		Our 18 pdr. batteries fired 80 rds during the day, mostly re-registration. Enemy's artillery were quiet except for a few 77mm.	
	15/11/15		Hostile artillery were very active during afternoon on our support trenches in vicinity of Embankment trench and also on Rue du Bois near Factory Corner apparently shooting at house used as O.P.s here. We retaliated heavily on houses suspected to be O.P.s and also on the Distillerie and effectively stopped hostile fire. 6 direct hits were made by 5.9" hows. on Carpet Factory which was formerly used for observation purposes but not latterly.	
	16/11/15		Very quiet day. Nothing noteworthy occurred.	
		3.35 pm	A hostile aeroplane was observed going west about 7000 ft up.	
	17/11/15		Light was good for observation during most of day. Registration of distant objects was carried out during the morning calling forth retaliation by 5.9" Hows on our trenches in front of Rue du Bois. This was effectively checked by salvoes from all batteries of the Group at 1 pm and 1.5 pm on S16 d 7.7 and S16 a 6.1. In the afternoon 5.9" hows fell in neighbourhood of Rue des Chavatte (7 rds) and 4.2" hows were active on Rue du Bois. Our batteries retaliated and stopped the 4.2" fire.	

1875 Wt. W593/826 1,000,000 4/15 J.B.C. & A. A.D.S.S./Forms/C. 2118.

Army Form C. 2118

Instructions regarding War Diaries and Intelligence Summaries are contained in F. S. Regs., Part II. and the Staff Manual respectively. Title Pages will be prepared in manuscript.

WAR DIARY
or
INTELLIGENCE SUMMARY
(Erase heading not required.)

Place	Date	Hour	Summary of Events and Information	Remarks and references to Appendices
	17/10/15	12.40 pm	The smoke of a train was seen at Lorgies	
	18/10/15		Some enemy shelling at 1.30 pm and 3 pm. ~~An~~ Salvoes by the Group on S18c 9.4 and S29 a 4.5 put a stop to this.	
	19/10/15		About noon 77mm and 4.2" shells fell on our trenches near Farm Corner (opposite Fme du Bois). Our batteries immediately retaliated on tender spots in the enemy's lines and rest of day passed quietly. Weather very misty.	
	20/10/15		Several Germans were seen at house S23 c 9.6 and house S23 b 2.6. Both these houses were shelled by B-88 who also dispersed a working party. Enemy's artillery were fairly quiet.	
	21/10/15	1.30 pm to 1.35 pm	The Carpet Factory was subjected to heavy shell fire by 4.2 how & 77mm. Again at dusk there was a certain amount of hostile shelling by 5.9" and 77mm. Observation was difficult owing to mist but salvoes were fired in retaliation on enemy's support and communication during afternoon. Sections of A and D Batteries were relieved about 5 pm by Sections of 1st and 2nd Lincs. Batteries	

1875 Wt. W593/826 1,000,000 4/15 J.B.C. & A. A.D.S.S./Forms/C. 2118.

Instructions regarding War Diaries and Intelligence Summaries are contained in F. S. Regs., Part II. and the Staff Manual respectively. Title Pages will be prepared in manuscript.

WAR DIARY
or
INTELLIGENCE SUMMARY
(Erase heading not required.)

Army Form C. 2118

Place	Date	Hour	Summary of Events and Information	Remarks and references to Appendices
	21/11/15		Sections of B and C batteries marched out to Rest Billets N.W. of St Venant. A & D batteries handed over guns and 18/pr dumped ammunition to incoming batteries.	19th Divnl Arty Instrns for Relief No. 11 19/11/15
	22/11/15	5 pm	Remaining sections of A & D relieved and remaining sections of B & C marched out. During day command of composite batteries was assumed by battery commanders of relieving batteries	
		4 pm	Command of Right Group was handed over to O.C. 1st North Midland Brigade RFA	46th Divnl Arty "Exchange of 18/pr equipment" No. 1211/4
Bas Hamel J 31, 32 & 27 c.	23/11/15		H.Q. Bde Amm. Col. and C-88 in rest at Bas Hamel. A, B & D-88 in rest at Les Amusoires (P 17) A & D 88 received new guns.	
	24/11/15		Section training by all Units commenced.	
	25/11/15		Carried on with section training overhauling guns etc	
	26/11/15		do.	
	27/11/15		do.	
	28/11/15		do.	
	29/11/15		do.	
	30/11/15		do.	

O Beal Lt
Adjt 88 F.A. Bde

1875 Wt. W593/826 1,000,000 4/15 J.B.C. & A. A.D.S.S./Forms/C. 2118.

SECRET COPY NO: 7...

46th: DIVISIONAL ARTILLERY

OPERATION ORDER NO: 25

November 5th: 1915

REFERENCE MAP - Combined Sheet BETHUNE

INFORMATION (1) The XIth: Corps less 12th: Division will relieve the Indian Corps. The 19th: Division will come under the Command of the XIth: Corps.

The 46th: Division will relieve the MEERUT Division and the LAHORE Division.

INFANTRY RELIEFS. (2) Night 6th:/7th: November

(a) 139th: Infantry Brigade takes over Trenches from MEERUT Division.

(b) MEERUT Divisional Artillery remains in its position in support of 139th: Infantry Brigade.

(c) G.O.C. 46th: Division assumes Command from G.O.C. MEERUT Division on Completion of Relief.

Night 10th:/11th: November.

(a) 137th: Infantry Brigade relieves LAHORE Division in the Trenches.

(b) LAHORE Divisional Artillery remains in its position in support of 137th: Infantry Brigade.

(c) G.O.C. 46th: Division takes over Command of the line on Completion of the Relief.

14th: November and Night 14th:/15th: November.

Guards Division take over the Left of Line held by 137th: Infantry Brigade as far as a Communication Trench, 15th: Street (S.5.c.9.9) inclusive.

ARTILLERY RELIEFS (3)

(a) The MEERUT Divisional Artillery and LAHORE Divisional Artillery will be relieved by 46th: Divisional Artillery as under, and according to attached schedule.

CONTINUED 2.

ARTILLERY RELIEFS (b) <u>Nights 8th:/9th: and 9th:/10th: November.</u>

Night 8th/9th and 9th/10th

C.89 (How:) Battery, 19th: Divisional Artillery will relieve 61st: (How:) Battery MEERUT Divisional Artillery.

Night 9th/10th and 10th/11th

(c) <u>Nights 9th:/10th: and 10th:/11th: November.</u>

One 18-Pr: Brigade (less 1 Battery) 19th: Divisional Artillery, and 1st: and 2nd: North Midland Brigades R.F.A. and 2nd: Derby (How:) Battery, 46th: Divisional Artillery, will relieve remainder of MEERUT Divisional Artillery

Night 11th/12th and 12th/13th

(d) <u>Nights 11th:/12th: and 12th:/13th: November.</u>

3rd: North Midland Brigade. R.F.A. and 1st: Derby: (How:) Battery, 46th: Divisional Artillery will relieve part of LAHORE Divisional Artillery.

COMMAND (4). G.O.C. R.A. 46th: Division will assume Command of the Artillery from completion of reliefs on and after 10th:/11th: November.

R.A. GROUPS (5) The O.C. 18-Pr: Brigade. R.F.A. from 19th: Divisional Artillery will take over Head Quarters of 4th: Brigade. R.F.A. MEERUT Division, and Command the Right Group.

3

The O.C. 2nd: North Midland Brigade. R.F.A. will take over the Head Quarters of 13th: Brigade. R.F.A. MEERUT Division and Command the Centre Group.

The O.C. 3rd: North Midland Brigade. R.F.A. will take over the Head Quarters of 11th: Brigade. R.F.A. LAHORE Division, and Command the Left Group.

The O.C. 1st: North Midland Brigade. R.F.A. will find suitable Head Quarters from which he can Command his own Brigade. Place selected to be reported as soon as possible.

The O.C. 4th: North Midland (How:) Brigade. R.F.A. will find a suitable Head Quarters from which to Command his Brigade. Place selected to be reported as soon as possible.

CONTINUED 3.

COMMUNICATIONS. 6 (6) Telephone Communications will be handed over intact. Instruments will not be handed over.

COMPLETION of RELIEFS. 7 (7) ~~Group~~ Battery Commanders will report by Telephono the completion of all reliefs, and whether the Communications are correct.

(8) R.A. Head Quarters will be established at FOSSE (R.22.a.4.5). at 12 Noon, Nov 7th

R. A. Budge
Brigade Major.
46th: Divisional Artillery.

COPY NO: ...... ISSUED AT ...7..a.m.

Xlth: Corps R.A.
Head Quarters
46th: Division (2 Copies).
Meerut Divisional Artillery.
Lahore Divisional Artillery.
19th: Divisional Artillery (3 Copies).
137th: Infantry Brigade.
138th: Infantry Brigade.
139th: Infantry Brigade.
O.C. 1st: North Midland Brigade. R.F.A.
2nd: North Midland Brigade. R.F.A.
3rd: North Midland Brigade. R.F.A.
4th: North Midland Brigade. R.F.A.
Divisional Ammunition Column.
Signals, 46th: Division.
S.S.O.
War Diary.

SECRET. Copy No. 4...

INSTRUCTIONS

MEERUT DIVISIONAL ARTILLERY.

INFANTRY RELIEFS. 1. The 46th Division will relieve the MEERUT and LAHORE Divisions.
The 139th Infantry Brigade takes over trenches from MEERUT Division on night 6th/7th November. G.O.C. 46th Division assumes command from G.O.C. MEERUT Division on completion of relief.
MEERUT Divisional Artillery remains on the line in support of the 139th Infantry Brigade.
The Sub-sections of the front will remain unaltered and batteries will continue to cover their present fronts.

ARTILLERY RELIEFS. 2. NIGHT 8th/9th November:-

1 Section 61st Howitzer Battery will be relieved by 1 Section C/89 Howitzer Battery, and will withdraw to its wagon line.

NIGHT 9th/10th November:-

Remaining 2 Sections 61st Howitzer Battery will be relieved by 1 Section C/89 Howitzer Battery, and will march to billets in the new area.
1 Section of each of the following batteries will be relieved by 1 Section of the batteries shown against them:-

7th Battery R.F.A.	by	A/88 Battery R.F.A.
66th Battery R.F.A.	by	C/88 Battery R.F.A.
14th Battery R.F.A.	by	1/Staffordshire Battery R.F.A.
44th Battery R.F.A.	by	3/ ,, ,,
8th Battery R.F.A.	by	2/ ,, ,,
2nd Battery R.F.A.	by	2/Lincolnshire Battery R.F.A.
60th(How)Btty R.F.A.	by	2/Derbyshire Battery R.F.A.

The above Sections on being withdrawn will go to their wagon lines.

NIGHT 10th/11th November:-

The remaining 2 Sections of the batteries shown above will be relieved by the remainder of the relieving batteries of 11th Corps and will march to billets in the new area.

NOTES:- The Section of the 61st Howitzer Battery which withdraws to its wagon line on the night 8th/9th November, and the Sections of all batteries which withdraw to their wagon lines on the night 9th/10th November, will march to their billets in the new area on the mornings of the 9th and 10th, respectively.
On Nights 9th/10th and 10th/11th November - B/88 Battery R.F.A. will go into the unoccupied position at S 2 c 6'7, and the 3/Lincolnshire Battery R.F.A. will go into the unoccupied position at M 31 b 4'2.

COMMAND. 3. Officers Commanding IND. III. and IND. IV. Artillery Groups will hand over command to the Officers Commanding 88th Brigade R.F.A.(19th Division) and 2nd North Midland Brigade R.F.A., respectively, at a time to be notified later.
G.O.C., R.A., MEERUT Division will hand over command of the Artillery on 139th Infantry Brigade front to G.O.C., R.A., 46th Division at a time to be notified later.

COMMUNICATIONS 4. All telephone communications will be handed over intact.

P.T.O.

AMMUNITION SUPPLY. 5. Brigade and Divisional Ammunition Columns will remain in their present positions and continue to supply ammunition until completion of reliefs on the night 10th/11th November. They will march to billets in the new area on the morning of the 11th November.
The 9th Brigade R.F.A. Ammunition Column will supply S.A.A. to the 139th Infantry Brigade until the supply is taken over by a Brigade Ammunition Column of the 46th Divisional Artillery.

REPORTS. 6. Reports to the CHATEAU at CROIX MARMEUSE.

Captain R.A.
for Brigade Major, Royal Artillery,
MEERUT DIVISION.

No.1505-R.A.(L).

6th November 1915.

Issued at 11.a.m.

Copy No. 1 to LAHORE Division.
,, 2 to MEERUT Division.
,, 3 to Brigadier General R.A., INDIAN Corps.
,, 4 to 19th Divisional Artillery.
,, 5 to 46th Divisional Artillery.
,, 6 to 139th Infantry Brigade.
,, 7 to BAREILLY Brigade.
,, 8. to DEHRA DUN Brigade.
,, 9 to 4th Brigade R.F.A.
,, 10 to 9th Brigade R.F.A.
,, 11 to 13th Brigade R.F.A.
,, 12 to 131st Howitzer Brigade R.F.A.
,, 13 to MEERUT Divisional Ammunition Column.
,, 14 to War Diary.
,, 15 to File.

S E C R E T. Copy No ..4.....

XIXth DIVISIONAL ARTILLERY.

OPERATION ORDER No 9.

7th November 1915.

1. "D"/89th (How) F.A. Brigade is placed under the orders of the 46th Division and will move to the new positions allotted to it by the 46th Divisional Artillery on the night 8th/9th November.

2. "A", "B" and "C" Batteries, 88th F.A.Brigade are placed under the orders of the 46th Division with effect from the 9th November inclusive.

AMMUNITION.

(a) The Ammunition supply of all the above will be arranged by 19th Divisional Artillery.

(b) Daily Ammunition Expenditure Return will be rendered to 46th Divisional Artillery.

(c) Weekly Ammunition Return will be sent to the 19th Divisional Artillery.

[illegible signature]

Major R.F.A.
Brigade Major R.A. 19th Division.

Issued at 6.30 p.m.

Copy No 1 to War Diary.
,, ,, 2 File
,, ,, 3 B.G. R.A., Indian Corps.
,, ,, 4 B.G.R.A., 11th Corps.
,, ,, 5 46th Divisional Artillery.
,, ,, 6 MEERUT Divisional Artillery.
,, ,, 7 88th F.A.Brigade.
,, ,, 8 89th F.A.Brigade.
,, ,, 9 IND.I. Artillery Group.
,, ,, 10 IND.II. Artillery Group.
,, ,, 11 19th Divisional Ammunition Column.
,, ,, 12 19th Division.

Extracts from orders of

Meerut ~~Divnl~~, 19th ~~Div~~ 46th Divnl Arty

H.Q.

Reliefs.

S C H E D U L E

of

ARTILLERY RELIEFS. 46th: DIVISIONAL ARTILLERY

--:--:--:--:--:--:--:--

REFERENCE - BETHUNE Combined Sheet

DATE.	BATTERY.	TO RELIEVE.	LOCATION.	REMARKS.
		RIGHT GROUP		
9th/10th and 10th/11th NOVEMBER	C.O.18-Pr: Bde:	C.O.4th:Bde:R.F.A.	LACOUTRE X.4.b.8.8	--
	1-18-Pr: (C 88) Battery	7th: Battery.	S.7.b.2.7	--
	1-18-Pr: (B 88) Battery	NO RELIEF.	To go into unoccupied position at ~~S.2.c.6.7~~ S 8 a 8.8.	To cover Left half of Front now covered by 7th:Bty R.F.A.
	1-18-Pr: (A 88) Battery	66th: Bty:R.F.A.	S.7.d.8.2	--
	1st:Staffs: Bty:	14th: Bty:R.F.A.	S.1.d.4.8	--
8th/9th and 9th/10th NOVEMBER	C/89 (How) Bty:	61st: Bty: R.F.A.	S.7.b.3.9	--
		CENTRE GROUP		
9th/10th and 10th/11th NOVEMBER	C.O.2nd:N.M.Bde:	C.O.13th:Bde:R.F.A	R.29.c.2.8	--
	3rd: Staffs: Bty:	44th: Bty:R.F.A.	M.32.c.10.6½	--
	2nd: Staffs: Bty:	8th: Bty: R.F.A.	M.31.b.10.6.	--
	2nd: Lincs: Bty:	2nd: Bty: R.F.A.	M.32.a.4.5	--
	3rd: Lincs: Bty:	NO RELIEF.	To go into unoccupied position at M.31.b.4.2	To cover Left half of front now covered by 2nd:Bty
	2nd: Derby: Bty:	60th: Bty: R.F.A.	S.32.b.5.5	--
		LEFT GROUP		
11th/12th and 12th/13th NOVEMBER	C.O.3rd:N.M.Bde:	C.O.11th:Bde:R.F.A.	R.24.a.5.9	--
	4th: Staffs: Bty:	93rd: Bty: R.F.A.	M.26.a.8.8	--
	5th: Staffs: Bty:	84th: Bty: R.F.A.	M.26.c.9.7	--
	6th: Staffs: Bty:	85th: Bty: R.F.A.	M.20.d.6.2	--
	1st: Derby: Bty:	NO RELIEF.	To go into unoccupied position at M.32.b.3.3	--

NOTE Batteries which relieve those with one or two detached Guns for Enfilade fire, will detach one Gun only.

Subject:- Exchange of 18 Pr: Equipment.

Headquarters,
46th: Division.
O.C.
1st: North Midland Brigade. R.F.A.
2nd: North Midland Brigade. R.F.A.
3rd: North Midland Brigade. R.F.A.
4th: North Midland Brigade. R.F.A.
88th: Brigade. R.F.A.

(1) Arrangements have been made for the following Batteries to exchange in Relief, Guns less Dial Sights, and Wagons which are built into Emplacements. Date will be notified later.

1st: Lincs: Battery with A/88 Battery.

2nd: Lincs: Battery with D/88 Battery.

3rd: Lincs: Battery with D/86 Battery.

The 1st: Derby: Battery will arrange to occupy the position of D/89 Battery.

(2) (a) The 1st: Lincs: Battery will not go into action until further orders, but will arrange to take over, and hand over Equipment as above, with the A/88 Battery.

(b) 2nd: and 3rd: Lincs: Batteries will withdraw from action their 15 Pr: Equipment in accordance with orders already issued, but they will not put any 18 Pr: Guns into action - they will make all arrangements for taking over, and handing over Equipment as detailed in paragraph (1) to their respective Batteries.

(3) 18 Pr: Ammunition dumped in Emplacements will be taken over as it stands.

(4) ZONES

O.C. 1st: North Midland Brigade. R.F.A. will be prepared to cover from S.22.c.3.1 to FME: du BOIS, and will reconnoitre at once for this purpose.

(5) From 4 p.m. tomorrow (19th: November) the Centre Group Commander will arrange to cover from FME du BOIS to the LA BASSEE Road.

The Left Group Commander will arrange to cover, from the same time, from the LA BASSEE Road to SIGN POST LANE.

CONTINUED (2).

ZONES

The Zone for the Right Group Commander remains unaltered.

(6) O.C. 4th: North Midland Brigade. R.F.A. will arrange for the 1st: Derby: Battery to cover from S.22.c.3.1 to S.16.a.3.7, and will reconnoitre at once for this purpose.

A.P. Burke
Brigade Major.
46th: Divisional Artillery.

H.Q. R.A.
18th: November, 1915.

S E C R E T.

Copy No ...9.....

XIXth DIVISIONAL ARTILLERY.

INSTRUCTIONS FOR RELIEF No 11.

19th November 1915.

Reference:- TRENCH MAP and
BETHUNE Combined Sheet.

1. On the nights 21st/22nd, 22nd/23rd instants, the 19th Divisional Artillery will be relieved as follows:-

(a) On the front from GRENADIER ROAD to LA QUINQUE RUE by the 7th Divisional Artillery.

(b) On the front from LA QUINQUE RUE to PIPE Communication Trench by the 46th Divisional Artillery.

On relief they will march into Reserve Billets under Brigade arrangements.

2. Night 21st/22nd November.

1 Section "C"/86th at S.7.d.5.0. hands over to 1 Section 105th Bty.
Detchd. Sect. "C"/87th at S.14.c.5.8. to 1 Section 105th Bty.
1 Section "A"/86th at X.24.c.3.9. to 1 Section 106th Bty.
1 Section "B"/87th at X.23.a.6.3. to 1 Section 106th Bty.
1 Section "A"/87th at X.22.d.6.6. to 1 Section 12 th Bty.

1 Section "A"/88th at S.7.d.6.3. to 1 Section 1st Lincs.Bty.
1 Section "D"/88th at S.7.d.8.7. to 1 Section 2nd Lincs.Bty.
1 Section "D"/86th at X.17.d.8.2. to 1 Section 3rd Lincs.Bty.
1 Section "D"/89th at X.18.A.32. to 1 Section 1st Derby Bty.

3. Night 22nd/23rd November.

Remaining Section "C"/86th hands over to 1 Section 105th Battery.
Remaining Section "A"/86th hands over to 1 Section 106th Battery.
Remaining Section ("C"/87th hands over to 2 Sections 12th Battery.
("A"/87th

Remaining Section "A"/88th hands over to 1 Section 1st Lincs. Battery.
Remaining Section "D"/88th hands over to 1 Section 2nd Lincs. Battery.
Remaining Section "D"/86th hands over to 1 Section 3rd Lincs. Battery.
Remaining Section "D"/89th hands over to 1 Section 1st Derby Battery.

Remaining Batteries and Sections of 19th Divisional Artillery pull out and march into Reserve Billets.

4. Batteries being relieved by the 7th Divisional Artillery will take out their guns and ammunition complete.

Those relieved by the 46th Divisional Artillery will leave their guns, wagons if dug in, and ammunition in pits, but will take out their dial sights No 1 with mirror attachment, under arrangements to be made between Brigades.

5. When marching to Reserve Billets, the 87th and 89th F.A. Brigades will proceed by route through X.8.c. - X.7.a. - W.6.b. - Q.30.a. - ROBECQ - St. VENANT.

The 86th F.A.Brigade by route through X.8.Central - X.1.d. - R.32.c. - Q.30.a. - Q.23.a. - CALONNE - St. VENANT.

The 88th F.A.Brigade by route through ZELOBES - PARADIS - CALONNE - CANAL BANK - St. VENANT.

6. The D.A.C. will march to Reserve Billets on the 23rd November, being clear of their present billets by 8.0 a.m.

7. Headquarters 19th Divisional Artillery will be at LOCON until 10.0 a.m. on the 22nd inst, when the G.O.Cs. R.A. 7th Divisional Artillery and 46th Divisional Artillery respectively take over Command of Artillery Groups.
After this hour, H.Q. R.A. 19th Division will be at P.5.b.3.10.

Noel Chance
Captain R.F.A.
for Brigade Major R.A. 19th Division.

Issued at 6.0 p.m.

Copies to:-
War Diary.
File.
C.R.A. XIth Corps.
19th Division. (3 copies)
IND.I. Artillery Group.
IND.II. Artillery Group.
88th F.A.Brigade.
89th F.A.Brigade.
19th Divisional Ammunition Column.
7th Divisional Artillery.
46th Divisional Artillery.
2nd Brigade R.G.A.
28th Siege Brigade R.G.A.
6th Kite and Balloon Section.
10th Squadron R.F.C.
56th Infantry Brigade.
57th Infantry Brigade.
58th Infantry Brigade.

These instructions are included in orders sent out to Battns on 20th

19th Div

Dec 1915

88th Bde: R.F.A.
Vol: 5

Instructions regarding War Diaries and Intelligence Summaries are contained in F. S. Regs., Part II. and the Staff Manual respectively. Title Pages will be prepared in manuscript.

WAR DIARY
or
INTELLIGENCE SUMMARY
(Erase heading not required.)

Army Form C. 2118

Place	Date	Hour	Summary of Events and Information	Remarks and references to Appendices
Bas Hamel	1/12/15		Section Training	[illegible]
	2/12/15		" "	[illegible]
	3/12/15		" "	[illegible]
	4/12/15		Brigade went into action. taking over from the 46th Divn. Reliefs were effected at 4 pm A/88 at S7.d.6.3 (Old position) B/88 X17a73. (Old D/86 position) C/88 S1.d.4.9 (Old Stafford position) D/88 S7 D.8.6 (Old O position) B/86 M32 D08. D/89 X18a.25. Enfilade Guns A/89 Pont Logy Position C/86 M34 c52. D/86 X14 a.2.0. Right Group Headquarters same house at La Couture X4.6.8.6 Major Torey took over command of the Right Group at 4 pm Zone covered by the Right Group is LA QUINQUE RUE to COPSE STREET (S10.c.9.5) the 58 Infantry Brigade is on our front. 'J' RHA. S7.b.2.6. 88 Bde A.C took up its old position at Les Lobes	[illegible]
La Couture X4.6.8.6	5/12/15		Registration	[illegible]
	6/12/15		Batteries completed Registration	[illegible]
	7/12/15		Artillery passed quiet day	[illegible]
	8/12/15		Offensive Operation at the Ferme du Bois by the Right Group very successful. Hostile artillery retaliated slightly on Rue de Bois, no damage	[illegible]
	9/12/15		Day passed very quietly, 4 Germans were seen working at their parapets	[illegible]

1875 Wt. W593/826 1,000,000 4/15 J.B.C. & A. A.D.S.S./Forms/C. 2118.

Army Form C. 2118

Instructions regarding War Diaries and Intelligence Summaries are contained in F. S. Regs., Part II. and the Staff Manual respectively. Title Pages will be prepared in manuscript.

WAR DIARY
or
INTELLIGENCE SUMMARY
(Erase heading not required.)

Place	Date	Hour	Summary of Events and Information	Remarks and references to Appendices
	9/12/15		Contd in front of Boars Head, wearing light blue or grey uniforms. Light too bad to distinguish what they were doing. one man walked about 50 Yards in a Westerly direction.	£
	10/12/15		Day passed quietly, weather too misty for observation	£
	11/12/15		Offensive operations carried out on German second line trenches & communication trenches throughout the day from 10 am to 4 pm. House in which a searchlight is reported at S17 a 4.6. was shelled by our Batteries and severely damaged.	£
	12/12/15	10.35am	Offensive operations on enemy communication trenches at S16 b 4. 1½. Combined offensive operations on 2nd & 3rd line trenches & communication trenches in Zone 10.45 am to 4 pm. enemy retaliated with 77mm & 5.9 How. on Princes Road and Whiskey Corner. Between 3.15 & 3.45 pm the smoke of a locomotive shunting in the cutting at T15 d 3.7 was clearly seen. The enemy are working on their second line of defence near Lorgies as several bodies of men with picks & shovels were seen in the neighbourhood.	£

1875 Wt. W593/826 1,000,000 4/15 J.B.C. & A. A.D.S.S./Forms/C. 2118.

Instructions regarding War Diaries and Intelligence Summaries are contained in F. S. Regs., Part II. and the Staff Manual respectively. Title Pages will be prepared in manuscript.

WAR DIARY
or
INTELLIGENCE SUMMARY
(Erase heading not required.)

Army Form C. 2118

Place	Date	Hour	Summary of Events and Information	Remarks and references to Appendices
	13/12/15		Enemy Artillery active from direction of La Tourelle, fired on our reserve trenches between Savoy & Rest, 5.9 How. active on Rue du Bois from Savoy to Teetotal Corner. Our Batteries retaliated on Green Mound S.22 a 5.8. No movement of enemy was observed during the bombardment. A portion of an enemy shell passed through the roof the Officers billet & another portion through the Sergeants billet at 'C' Battery.	[illegible]
	14/12/15		Offensive operations by our Artillery, a considerable amount of damage done to enemy's trenches & wire. The enemy's fire through the day was much more severe, one 5.9" shell fell a direct hit into the sandbags of the Leicester Lounge but failed to detonate. At 1 pm the smoke of an engine was seen behind Illies.	[illegible]
	15/12/15		To days operation on the Green Mound was very satisfactory. A 9.2" Howitzer obtained 3 direct hits forming large craters in both N. and S. faces. The first hit by the 9.2" How. was very promptly followed up by the Field Batteries and as a result of the combined	[illegible]

Contd.

1875 Wt. W593/826 1,000,000 4/15 J.B.C. & A. A.D.S.S./Forms/C. 2118.

Army Form C. 2118

Instructions regarding War Diaries and Intelligence Summaries are contained in F. S. Regs., Part II. and the Staff Manual respectively. Title Pages will be prepared in manuscript.

WAR DIARY
or
INTELLIGENCE SUMMARY
(Erase heading not required.)

Place	Date	Hour	Summary of Events and Information	Remarks and references to Appendices
	15/12/15		bombardment the South face was breached right through. Upon subsequent examination the Green Mound appears to be a hollow rectangle, in which water can be seen. There are no indications that it is specially prepared for defence. The colour of the mound is now brown instead of green. The enemy retaliated with field guns on our trenches at S15c and a few 77mm shells fell in the neighbourhood of Chocolate Menier Corner S14 b 8.3. A 77mm battery obtained a direct hit on the top of the Trocadero	J
	16/12/15		Very little firing today, mist bad for observation.	J
	17/12/15		Weather & light very bad. Enemy 77mm Gun shelling our support trenches in front of Leicester Lounge. Hostile fire ceased after retaliation by our field Batteries	J

1875 Wt. W593/826 1,000,000 4/15 J.B.C. & A. A.D.S.S./Forms/C. 2118.

WAR DIARY
or
INTELLIGENCE SUMMARY

(*Erase heading not required.*)

Instructions regarding War Diaries and Intelligence Summaries are contained in F. S. Regs., Part II. and the Staff Manual respectively. Title Pages will be prepared in manuscript.

Army Form C. 2118

Place	Date	Hour	Summary of Events and Information	Remarks and references to Appendices
	18/12/15	11-20 to 11-40	Enemy shelled support trenches in front of SAVOY but soon ceased after retaliation by Field Batteries.	[illegible]
			Progress being made with strengthening O.P. [illegible]	
	20/12/15	10am	Enemy fired about 50 rounds at RICHEBOURG L'AVOUE.	[illegible]
			J.R.H.A commenced wire cutting operations but results difficult to observe owing to bad light.	
		9-30	3 Hostile Aeroplanes observed over S. 1d. 4.9 but returned to their own lines upon being fired at. Enemy 77mm shelled trenches in front of RUE DU BOIS & a 4.2 shelled O.P.s in neighbourhood of CHOCOLATE MENIER CORNER	
	21/12/15	10-0am	Wire cutting operations continued but although wire was considerably knocked about nothing definite can be gathered as to what extent as observation was impossible. Enemy evidently annoyed by operations as they retaliated more than usual.	[illegible]
		8.15 to 9.15pm	Batteries opened fire on selected targets as German relief was suspected.	
	22/12/15		Wire cutting operations again continued with good results, Retaliation from enemy rather quiet. Light bad for observation. Some red rockets were seen in the direction of RUE d'OUVERT	[illegible]

1875 Wt. W593/826 1,000,000 4/15 J.B.C. & A. A.D.S.S./Forms/C. 2118.

Instructions regarding War Diaries and Intelligence Summaries are contained in F. S. Regs., Part II. and the Staff Manual respectively. Title Pages will be prepared in manuscript.

WAR DIARY
or
INTELLIGENCE SUMMARY
(Erase heading not required.)

Army Form C. 2118

Place	Date	Hour	Summary of Events and Information	Remarks and references to Appendices
	23/12/15	9-10	Batteries of the group opened fire on night lines with a view to finding out if these could be improved upon. They were found to be generally sound but certain adjustments to them have now been made. An attempt was made to repair the wire cut about S.10.c.8½.4 but the party were soon dispersed by our fire.	[illegible]
	24/12/15		Houses about LORGIES were shelled heavily from about 11-10 to 11-45 am as some movement has been observed there of late. On the days offensive operations the fire appeared very effective & many burst well in amongst houses. Enemy retaliation was not excessive, a good deal of fire however took place at various places during the afternoon. During the ~~evening~~ & night we fired at intervals, at 5pm to 8pm, 1-5am to 1.20am 5am to 6am & every 10 minutes up till daylight to annoy & destroy enemy who are believed to be billetted at LORGIES & LA. TOURELL X Roads.	[illegible]
	25/12/15		Enemy's 77 mm fairly active on RUE DU BOIS & Reserve Trenches during the morning. Night operations of previous night repeated.	[illegible]
	26/12/15		Field guns were not as active as usual. New communication trench at S.16.d.7.7 has been added to considerably during the last few days. Enemy's working parties could be seen there today. Wire cut by J/R.H.A. at point 8.1. has been partially repaired during the night.	[illegible]

1875 Wt. W593/826 1,000,000 4/15 J.B.C. & A. A.D.S.S./Forms/C. 2118.

Instructions regarding War Diaries and Intelligence Summaries are contained in F. S. Regs., Part II. and the Staff Manual respectively. Title Pages will be prepared in manuscript.

Army Form C. 2118

WAR DIARY
or
INTELLIGENCE SUMMARY
(Erase heading not required.)

Place	Date	Hour	Summary of Events and Information	Remarks and references to Appendices
	27/12/15		About 50 enemy shells 8" were fired today at Richebourg Church. There were 12 or 13 direct hits, one of which demolished the upper portion of the Tower. In addition to the larger shells there were a considerable number of (probably 5.9) fired. Considerable damage was done to buildings but the line & range for the Church was extraordinarily accurate.	
			What looks like a Machine Gun emplacement was observed at W corner of house at S.22 b 6.1. The 56th Infantry Brigade relieved the 57th Infantry Brigade, relief complete at 10.35 pm	
			8" & 77 mm shelled intermittently throughout the day.	[initialled]
	28/12/15		Section of C/86 lent to the Group for wire cutting purposes. Commenced to cut wire at about S.16.a 6.9. Other Batteries of the Group opened heavy fire on selected targets with the object of distracting the attention of the enemy from wire cutting guns. The result of wire cutting operations were good & a lane was cut	
			C/86 wirecutting gun returned to own unit	[initialled]
			Enemy's retaliation was very slight. Climatic conditions cloudy, but fine for short ranges	
	29/12/15	10a.	Commenced Registering Targets by Aeroplane, few targets registered as Hostile Aeroplane interrupted the work. An enemy machine gun emplacement was accurately located at S.16a 6.6. Enemy continually shelled O.Ps from 1.20 to 3.20 pm. There were 3 direct hits on the GAIETY but it is still serviceable for observation. 15 of the last shells fired at Gaiety were blind	[initialled]
	30/12/15		Enemy again shelled our OPs but firing was subdued about 2.30 pm by our batteries. Rest of day rather quiet. Weather cloudy but misty & bad for observation for distances	[initialled]

1875 Wt. W593/826 1,000,000 4/15 J.B.C. & A. A.D.S.S./Forms/C. 2118.

Army Form C. 2118

WAR DIARY

or

INTELLIGENCE SUMMARY

(Erase heading not required.)

Instructions regarding War Diaries and Intelligence Summaries are contained in F. S. Regs., Part II. and the Staff Manual respectively. Title Pages will be prepared in manuscript.

Place	Date	Hour	Summary of Events and Information	Remarks and references to Appendices
	31.12.15		The 7th LONDON ~~BRIGADE~~ BATTERY, R.F.A., which has been in action with Right Artillery Group 19th Divisional Artillery for the past 10 days, withdrew into rest at [illegible].	[illegible]

1875 Wt. W593/826 1,000,000 4/15 J.B.C. & A. A.D.S.S./Forms/C. 2118.

B

88th Bde: RFA.

Vol 7

Army Form C. 2118.

WAR DIARY
or
INTELLIGENCE SUMMARY
(Erase heading not required.)

Instructions regarding War Diaries and Intelligence Summaries are contained in F. S. Regs., Part II. and the Staff Manual respectively. Title Pages will be prepared in manuscript.

Place	Date	Hour	Summary of Events and Information	Remarks and references to Appendices
La Couture	1/1/16		In the morning the Group Artillery attacked three buildings suspected O.P.'s within the group zone. Much damage was done to buildings. Enemy shelling & retaliation throughout the day was light.	
	2/1/16		From 2 to 3 pm the Group Artillery fired short bursts of fire on their night objective, with the object of ascertaining by observation the collective fire of the Group whether the objectives have been suitably selected. It was found that the collective fire of the Group on night objectives creates an efficient barrage. Enemy retaliation was light. Our Batteries are now firing an average about 100 rounds per Battery per day. The Germans are firing on our front about one third the weight of shell that we are.	
	3/1/16		The ordinary work of the Group was carried out on the initiative of B.C.'s. About 300 rounds fired. Two objectives were registered by aeroplane observation.	
	4/1/16		No change. About 350 rounds fired by the Group Artillery on initiative of B.C.'s	
	5/1/16		In the morning the Group Artillery 4.5 How + 18 prs attacked three groups of buildings in the German lines with satisfactory results. We fired about 560 rounds. Enemy retaliation not severe.	
	6/1/16		Ordinary work of the Group. About 200 rounds fired. To day & during night 6th/7th the 113 Infantry Brigade 38th Div relieved the 56th Infantry Brigade 19th Div on the Group front. Detachments from four Batteries 38th Div Arty are now attached to Batteries of the Group for instruction in fire discipline & fire tactics since 31/12/15.	
	7/1/16		Group programme carried out between 11.40 am & 1.10 pm. Two guns C/86 lent by 86th Bde R.F.A. very successfully cut wire & destroyed parapet about S.16.a.7.9½ Trench Map 1/10000. About 40 yards of wire + parapet destroyed. Maj Wilson C/88 Battery observed from front line trench. Range 1400 yards. Group Batteries simultaneously destroyed section of German parapet on our front.	

Instructions regarding War Diaries and Intelligence Summaries are contained in F. S. Regs., Part II. and the Staff Manual respectively. Title Pages will be prepared in manuscript.

WAR DIARY
or
INTELLIGENCE SUMMARY
(Erase heading not required.)

Army Form C. 2118

Place	Date	Hour	Summary of Events and Information	Remarks and references to Appendices
	8/1/16		No Change. Enemy shelled Richebourg St Vaaste systematically with 5.9 from 11am to 2pm. A direct hit, field gun, emplacement of single enfilade gun C/86 attached to D/88. one killed, two wounded.	
	9/1/16		No Change. Enemy shelled La Couture about every three minutes from 11.15am to 4.15pm with 8" + 5.9 Three direct hits on East End of Church one of these was blind. A fair amount of damage done to houses near Church. The remarkable thing was that nearly all the 5.9 fired were blind & a fair number of 8". Retaliated on Lorgies	
	10/1/16		No Change. Wire cutting operation at S.10.c.9.5. four lanes were cut 110 rounds expended Group Batteries simultaneously destroyed parapet + houses suspected in O.P.'s	
	11/1/16		Smoke demonstration carried out with object of killing Germans by Artillery fire at daybreak 7am, about 400 rounds expended. At 3.30pm a section of C/86 attempted to cut wire at point S.16.a.3.7 other Batteries of the Group opened fire on selected objectives & a bombing party at 5pm through bombs over the German parapet, result not known	
	12/1/16		No Change. Ordinary work of Group carried out.	
	13/1/16		No Change. Ordinary work of Group carried out.	
	14/1/16		No Change An attempt at Wire Cutting at S.16.c.6.4. Enemy artillery unusually quiet	
	15/1/16		No Change Continuation of Wire Cutting operation on South Face of Boar Head Retaliation was more severe than usual	
	16/1/16		No Change Continuation Wire Cutting S.16.c.5.4 + 5.2. Enemy shelled two of our aeroplanes at long range some of the pieces of shell falling near La Couture.	
	17/1/16		No Change Wire Cutting with section of D/121 Battery + Group Batteries distracting attention from wire cutting section. Enemy retaliation more severe than usual	

1875 Wt. W593/826 1,000,000 4/15 J.B.C. & A. A.D.S.S./Forms/C. 2118.

Instructions regarding War Diaries and Intelligence Summaries are contained in F. S. Regs., Part II. and the Staff Manual respectively. Title Pages will be prepared in manuscript.

WAR DIARY
or
INTELLIGENCE SUMMARY
(Erase heading not required.)

Army Form C. 2118

Place	Date	Hour	Summary of Events and Information	Remarks and references to Appendices
La Couture	18/1/16		No Change	
	19/1/16		-"- Enemy aeroplane very active during morning. A Railway engine was seen S.E. of Lorgies, also parties from train continued to march towards Lorgies.	
	20/1/16		No Change Ordinary work of Group Carried out. Several Trains were seen during day proceeding from Don towards Illies.	
	21/1/16		No Change Ordinary work of Group Carried out.	
	22/1/16		Infantry attempted a bombing attack at 6.12 pm on Southern face of Boars Head Salient but was cancelled owing to the Salient being more strongly held than usual. Batteries stood to arms from 6.12 pm till 9.30 pm.	
	23/1/16		No Change Ordinary work of Group Carried out.	
	24/1/16		-"- -"- -"- -"- -"- Enemy lit smoke candles at S.22.c.3.4 nothing unusual happened	
	25/1/16		D/121 fired 170 H.E + 70 Shrapnel at point of German Salient opposite Boars Head range about 1500, very successful 30 yards parapet to N.E was broken down & wire considerably knocked about. Enemy retaliation during operation very feeble. Batteries of the Group carried out an offensive operation on Front Second & Com. Trenches to distract attention from wire cutting section of D/121. Much Aircraft activity on both sides throughout day.	
	26/1/16		No Change Ordinary work of Group Carried out	
	27/1/16		-"- The Enemy shelled our Front Second & Reserve Trenches & as far back as the	

1875 Wt. W593/826 1,000,000 4/15 J.B.C. & A. A.D.S.S./Forms/C. 2118.

Instructions regarding War Diaries and Intelligence Summaries are contained in F. S. Regs., Part II. and the Staff Manual respectively. Title Pages will be prepared in manuscript.

WAR DIARY
or
INTELLIGENCE SUMMARY
(Erase heading not required.)

Army Form C. 2118

Place	Date	Hour	Summary of Events and Information	Remarks and references to Appendices
	27/1/16	contd	Rue du Bois from 11am to 1.2pm with 77mm 4.2 Hows 5.9 Hows no doubt in celebration of the Kaiser's birthday. very little damage appears to have been done. the Group retaliated fairly heavily.	
	28/1/16		Wire cutting commenced 12.30 by D/121st Battery - results good, 3 lanes appeared to be cut at S.16a 4½ 7½ & enemy parapet badly damaged. New work done recently 20 yards N.E. of the point of the Salient completely demolished	
	29/1/16		One section of each Battery & Ammn. Column, relieved by one section 120th Brigade RFA moved back to rest billets. Guns etc being exchanged with 120th Brigade	
	30/1/16		Remaining sections relieved & moved back to rest billets. Command of Right Group handed over to C.C. 120th Brigade R.F.A. at 10am 31/12/15. One Subaltern, 3 telephonists & 2 N.C.O.s per battery left with relieving Batteries & 3 telephonists left at Hd-Qrs.	
	31/1/16		Batteries commenced training & smartening up of equipment generally.	

K. Army Lt

1875 Wt. W593/826 1,000,000 4/15 J.B.C. & A. A.D.S.S./Forms/C. 2118.

Instructions regarding War Diaries and Intelligence Summaries are contained in F. S. Regs., Part II. and the Staff Manual respectively. Title Pages will be prepared in manuscript.

WAR DIARY
or
INTELLIGENCE SUMMARY
(Erase heading not required.)

Army Form C. 2118

Place	Date	Hour	Summary of Events and Information	Remarks and references to Appendices
BAS HAMEL	1.2.16		Brigade training & smartening up of equipment generally whilst in rest billets	
J.31.c.2.8	2.2.16		-do- -do- -do-	
	3.2.16		-do- -do- -do-	
	4.2.16		-do- -do- -do-	
	5.2.16		-do- -do- Divisional Signal Exercise	
	6.2.16		-do- -do-	
	7.2.16		-do- -do-	
	8.2.16		-do- -do-	
	9.2.16		-do- -do- - Inspected at billets by G.O.C. R.A. 19th Div	
	10.2.16		-do- -do-	
	11.2.16		-do- -do-	
	12.2.16		Brigade turned out in Field Service Marching Order & marched past the G.O.C. 19th Div	
	13.2.16		Brigade training	
	14.2.16		" "	
	15.2.16		Two Officers & 5 telephonists per Battery & 5 telephonists from H.Q sent up to the Guards Divisional Arty, preparatory to this Brigade relieving them.	
	16.2.16		Brigade training	
	17.2.16		Four Guns & two ammunition wagons per Battery sent up together with sufficient personnel to take over & man guns of Guards Div Arty.	
Rue de Paradis LAVANTIE M.4.c.1.1.	18.2.16		Remaining vehicles & personnel moved up to new position, guns were exchanged with G. Div Arty & relief completed at 6 p.m & called New Left Group 19th Div Arty (consisting)	

1875 Wt. W593/826 1,000,000 4/15 J.B.C. & A. A.D.S.S./Forms/C. 2118.

Instructions regarding War Diaries and Intelligence Summaries are contained in F. S. Regs., Part II. and the Staff Manual respectively. Title Pages will be prepared in manuscript.

WAR DIARY
or
INTELLIGENCE SUMMARY
(Erase heading not required.)

Army Form C. 2118

Place	Date	Hour	Summary of Events and Information	Remarks and references to Appendices
LAVANTIE M.4.c.1.1.	18.2.16		(continued) consisting of A.B.C.D. Batteries 88th Brigade R.F.A. 88th Bde A.C. A/89 Battery Howitzer R.F.A. & 1 section of 89th Bde A.C. Position of Group H.Q + Batteries are as follows L.G. H.Q. M.4.c.1.1. A/88 Battery M.34.c.3½.4. B/88 M.21a.7.1. C/88 M.15.B.2.2. D/88 M.6.c.0.2. 88th/B.A.C R.3.c.8.2. A/89 M.15.d.1.1.	
	19.2.16		Registration	
	20.2.16		-do- + Scheme in conjunction with A.58 + No 4 Trench Mortar Batteries Front Line about M.36.a.5.6. + 5.9.	
	22/2/16		An unusually quite day characterised by entire absence of activity on the part of the enemy either in work or shelling. Very little sniping. Light bad throughout the day rendering observation impossible except at short intervals.	
	23/2/16		Scheme in conjunction with No 4 + A/58 Trench Mortar Batteries carried out with the object of damaging German Front Line trenches at M.36.A.5.5 + M.30.c.5.3. Enemy slow in retaliating but retaliation was fairly severe when it did start.	
	24/2/16		Fairly quiet day. Batteries continued registration + verifying targets taken over.	
	25/2/16		Group scheme arranged with Trench Mortar Batteries for damaging front line trenches + suspected Machine Gun emplacement at M.36.A.5.5 but only partly carried out owing to communication being broken down + T.M. not firing.	
	26/2/16		Hostile Fire rather more than usual throughout the day. Light bad for observation. A very strongly made cupola with a steel top apparently a machine gun emplacement located about M.36.A.5.7½.	

1875 Wt. W593/826 1,000,000 4/15 J.B.C. & A. A.D.S.S./Forms/C. 2118.

Army Form C. 2118

Instructions regarding War Diaries and Intelligence Summaries are contained in F. S. Regs., Part II. and the Staff Manual respectively. Title Pages will be prepared in manuscript.

WAR DIARY
or
INTELLIGENCE SUMMARY
(Erase heading not required.)

Place	Date	Hour	Summary of Events and Information	Remarks and references to Appendices
	27/2/16		Offensive operation carried out in conjunction with Trench Mortar Batteries on buildings & works in German 1st & 2nd Lines & rear which appeared effective & produced heavy retaliation. Enemy parapet in 2nd Line between M35.d.10.3 & M.36.A.3.0 badly damaged.	
	28/2/16		A gap about 30 yards broad was cut in enemy's wire about M.30.A.9.6 & parapet behind it levelled to the ground by D/87 Battery. Other Batteries of the group fired on selected objectives in 1st & 2nd Line & in rear	
	29/2/16		Ordinary work of the Group carried out. Many of the German 2nd Line & communication trenches show signs of new revetting especially those around MOULIN DU PIETRE. A German Aeroplane was brought down near PARADIS & the observer surrendered to an N.C.O of A/88 & a Sergt of the Yorkshire Dragoons	

H. Pooley. Lt Col RFA
Comdg 88th Bde RFA

1875 Wt. W593/826 1,000,000 4/15 J.B.C. & A. A.D.S.S./Forms/C. 2118.

Instructions regarding War Diaries and Intelligence Summaries are contained in F. S. Regs., Part II. and the Staff Manual respectively. Title Pages will be prepared in manuscript.

WAR DIARY
or
INTELLIGENCE SUMMARY
(Erase heading not required.)

Army Form C. 2118

Place	Date	Hour	Summary of Events and Information	Remarks and references to Appendices
LAVENTIE	1/3/16		Ordinary work of Group	
	2.3.16		" " " " ~~a German Aeroplane brought down near [illegible] pilot surrendered to an N.C.O. of A/88 Bty~~	
	3.3.16		" " " "	
	4.3.16		Attacked the German Salient in M.30.A in conjunction with II Corps Siege Group + Trench Mortar Batteries with the object of inflicting loss on the enemy	
	5.3.16		Ordinary work of Group	
	6.3.16		" " " "	
	7.3.16		" " " "	
	8.3.16		" " " "	
	9.3.16		Wire cutting by a section of D/87 at a range about 2000 x. the Batteries + Trench Mortar fired simultaneously to screen the wire cutting section.	
	10.3.16		Attempt to cut wire at M.24.D.4½.2. with a section of D/87 was repeated today. The results were rather disappointing as though a great deal of wire was knocked about no defined lanes were cut. The Enemy retaliated for combined shoot rather heavily with 5.9 + 77 mm.	
	11.3.16		Ordinary work of Group	
	12.3.16		" " " " (enemy aeroplane brought down at M.6.C.4.7. both occupants were unhurt)	
	13.3.16		" " " "	
	14.3.16		An intense Bombardment of our front line + support trenches between 11.10 am + 12.15 pm about 3000 rounds fired. B/87 Battery R.F.A joined the Group + came into action at M.16.D.5.9. A/159 B/159 C/159 D/159 Battery R.F.A joined the Group + took over from A/88 B/88 C/88 D/88 respectively (guns being exchanged) A/88 moved forward to M.17.A.7.4. B/88 to M.17.C.7.3. D/88 to M.17.A.5.1. C/88 a section to Neuve Chapelle M.35.C.3.6. one gun in front line trench at M.24.C.9.3 & one in F.L.T. at M.29.D.8.10. this was great work by C/88 Battery (Maj Wilson) considering the difficulties + labour this entailed. (Preparative to an offensive operation by the Division)	
	15.3.16		Wire cutting by section D/87 Battery was fairly satisfactory at M.30.A.5.5.	
	16.3.16		Ordinary work of Group	
	17.3.16		" " " "	
	18.3.16		" " " "	

W. Toovey Lt Col RFA
Comdg 88th Bde RFA

1875 Wt. W59[illegible]826 1,000,000 4/15 J.B.C. & A. A.D.S.S./Forms/C. 2118.

Instructions regarding War Diaries and Intelligence Summaries are contained in F. S. Regs., Part II. and the Staff Manual respectively. Title Pages will be prepared in manuscript.

WAR DIARY
or
INTELLIGENCE SUMMARY

(Erase heading not required.)

Army Form C. 2118

Place	Date	Hour	Summary of Events and Information	Remarks and references to Appendices
LAVENTIE	19.3.16		Ordinary work of Group	
	20.3.16		" " " Mining + Bombing operation successfully carried out	
	21.3.16		" " "	
	22.3.16		" " " A/159. B/159 C/159 D/159 Batteries withdrawn from the Group. A/88 B/88/ C/88/D/88 took over their old position. Divisional offensive operation being postponed.	
	23.3.16		Ordinary work of Group very little firing done owing to snow falling most of the day. B/87 + D/87 withdrawn from the Group.	
	24.3.16		Ordinary work of Group	
	25.3.16		Enemy Artillery particularly aggressive throughout the day. Our Tunnelling Company blew up a hostile mine gallery just in time to prevent the enemy exploding his mine	
	26.3.16		Enemy Trench Mortars active on our front line	
	27.3.16		Ordinary work of Group	
	28.3.16		" " "	
	29.3.16		" " "	
	30.3.16		" " "	
	31.3.16		" " " A/88 moved into position at M.16.D.6.9. + 1 Section of D/88 went into action in the Rue Logy position of A/88	

[illegible] Lt Col RFA
Comdg 88th Bde RFA.
1.4.16.

1875 Wt. W593/826 1,000,000 4/15 J.B.C. & A. A.D.S.S./Forms/C. 2118.

19

88th Bde: RFA.
Vol: 6

Instructions regarding War Diaries and Intelligence Summaries are contained in F. S. Regs., Part II. and the Staff Manual respectively. Title Pages will be prepared in manuscript.

WAR DIARY
or
INTELLIGENCE SUMMARY
(Erase heading not required.)

XIV

Army Form C. 2118

Vol 9

88 RFA

Place	Date	Hour	Summary of Events and Information	Remarks and references to Appendices
ZAVENTIE	1/4/16		Ordinary work of Group D/88 Battery heavily shelled 118 Infantry Brigade took over from 57 Infantry Brigade on our front (Moated Grange Sector)	
	2.4.16		Ordinary work of Group	
	3.4.16		" " "	
	4.4.16		" " "	
	5.4.16		" " " Rapid rate of fire maintained on selected objectives for one minute at 7.40pm unsuspected German relief	
	6.4.16		" " "	
	7.4.16		" " " 57 Infantry Brigade relieved the 118 Infantry Brigade in the Moated Grange Sector	
	8.4.16		" " "	
	9.4.16		" " "	
	10.4.16		" " " + registration with aeroplane	
	11.4.16		" " "	
	12.4.16		" " "	
	13.4.16		" " "	
	14.4.16		~~Brigade~~ One section per Battery relieved by 120 Brigade at 12 noon, the relieved section moving back into old Rest Billets at Bas Hamel - HAVERSKERQUE (guns being exchanged)	
	15.4.16		Remainder of Brigade moved back, relief being completed by 4.30pm.	
	16.4.16		Cleaning + Smartening up. Kit inspection	
	17.4.16		No change.	
	18.4.16		- " -	
	19.4.16		- " - B.A.C. inspected by G.O.C. R.A. 19th Div	

1875 Wt. W593/826 1,000,000 4/15 J.B.C. & A. A.D.S.S./Forms/C. 2118.

Army Form C. 2118

WAR DIARY
or
INTELLIGENCE SUMMARY
(Erase heading not required.)

Instructions regarding War Diaries and Intelligence Summaries are contained in F. S. Regs., Part II. and the Staff Manual respectively. Title Pages will be prepared in manuscript.

Place	Date	Hour	Summary of Events and Information	Remarks and references to Appendices
~~KAVANTIE~~	20th		No Change.	
BAS HAMEL	21st		Brigade Marched into 1st Army Training Area & Billets taken about DELETTE.	
DELETTE.	22nd		Brigade Training commenced	
	23rd		" ------- do ---------	
	24th		-------- do --------	
	26th		-------- do -------- & Divisional Signal exercise for Signallers	
	27th		Divisional Training	
	28th		Brigade Training & long distance signalling with Signal Coy.	
	29th		-------- do ----------------- do ---------------	
	30th		Divisional Training	

[signature] Lieut: Col:

Commanding 38th Brigade R.F.A.

1875 Wt. W593/826 1,000,000 4/15 J.B.C. & A. A.D.S.S./Forms/C. 2118.

Instructions regarding War Diaries and Intelligence Summaries are contained in F. S. Regs., Part II. and the Staff Manual respectively. Title Pages will be prepared in manuscript.

WAR DIARY
or
INTELLIGENCE SUMMARY
(Erase heading not required.)

Army Form C. 2118

88 RFA
Vol. 10

Place	Date	Hour	Summary of Events and Information	Remarks and references to Appendices
DELETTE	1/5/16		Brigade Training continued	
	2/5/16		Tactical Exercise carried out in conjunction with 58th Infantry Brigade	
	3/5/16		Brigade Training	
	4/5/16		Tactical Exercise in conjunction with Infantry	
	5/5/16		Exercise of previous day repeated but without guns & Infantry as practice for signallers	
	6/5/16		Brigade Training	
	7/5/16		Ordinary Work carried out	
	8/5/16		" " " & in evening Batteries marched to BERGUETTE Station to entrain for new area	
	9/5/16		Headquarters, 'A' & 'B' Batteries & ½ B.A.C arrived at new area & billets were taken in BELLOY	
	10/5/16		Remainder of the Brigade arrived & also took up billets in same village.	
BELLOY	11/5/16		Further Brigade Training commenced	
	12/5/16		— " — " contd	
	13/5/16		— " — "	
	14/5/16		— " — "	
	15/5/16		— " — "	
	16/5/16		— " — "	
	17/5/16		— " — "	
	18/5/16		" — " — " & 88th Brigade Ammunition Column abolished	
	19-24th		" — " — "	
	25/5/16		" — " — " & D/88th Battery was replaced by D/89th Battery making 3-18pdr	
	26th to 29th		" — " — " Batteries & 1-4.5" Howitzer Battery in the Brigade	
	30/5/16		Brigade marched into St RIQUIER Training area, near ABBEVILLE, & billets were taken in the neighbourhood of CAOURS	

1875 Wt. W593/826 1,000,000 4/15 J.B.C. & A. A.D.S.S./Forms/C. 2118.

[signature] R.F.A.

Army Form C. 2118

XIX

88 Bde RFA

June

Vol 11

Instructions regarding War Diaries and Intelligence Summaries are contained in F. S. Regs., Part II. and the Staff Manual respectively. Title Pages will be prepared in manuscript.

WAR DIARY
or
INTELLIGENCE SUMMARY
(Erase heading not required.)

Place	Date	Hour	Summary of Events and Information	Remarks and references to Appendices
CADURS	1/6/16		Brigade Training commenced in conjunction with 57th Infantry Brigade	
	2/6/16		" "	
	3/6/16		" "	
	4/6/16		Ordinary Parades carried out - remainder of day holiday	
	5/6/16		Brigade Training in conjunction with 57th Infantry Brigade continued	
	6/6/16		" "	
	7/6/16		" "	
	8/6/16		Signalling exercise for Brigade Hd-Qrs only - Remainder Gun-drill etc in billets	
	9/6/16		Divisional Scheme in conjunction with 89th Brigade RFA & 57th & 58th Infantry Brigades carried out	
	10/6/16		Firing Practice for A & B Batteries. 'C' Battery marched back to BELLOY	
	11/6/16		Hd-Qrs, 'A', 'B' & 'D' Batteries marched back to BELLOY & took up old billets there	
BELLOY	12/6/16		Ordinary Parades carried out	
	13/6/16		Hd-Qrs, A/88 & B/88 Batteries marched to BEHENCOURT & took billets there	
BEHENCOURT	14/6/16		Firing Practice carried out by 'A' & 'B' Batteries	
	15/6/16		" "	
	16/6/16		" " D/88 Battery also came to BEHENCOURT ×	× C/88 & D/88 Batteries are now attached to 87th & 89th Bdes respectively for tactical purposes
	17/6/16		Ordinary Parades carried out. Digging Party sent forward to neighbourhood of ALBERT	
	18/6/16		" "	
	19/6/16		" "	
	20/6/16		" & Party of Officers & Men from Hd-Qrs, A/88, & B/88 Batteries sent forward for reconnaissance work in neighbourhood of ALBERT. Small camp formed near DERNACOURT.	
	23/6/16		Remainder of Hd-Qrs, 'A' & B Batteries moved up to camp near DERNACOURT & work commenced in bridging trenches etc, preparatory to an advance on German Line.	
	24th to 30th		This work continued & completed as far as possible. Advance arranged to commence on 31st inst.	

30.6.16 [illegible] Lt Col RFA
Comdg 88th Bde RFA

1875 Wt. W593/826 1,000,000 4/15 J.B.C. & A. A.D.S.S./Forms/C. 2118.

19th Div.
III.Corps.

WAR
DIARY

Headquarters.

88th BRIGADE, R.F.A.

J U L Y

1 9 1 6

Attached:

Report on Operations
night of 17th/18th.

Instructions regarding War Diaries and Intelligence Summaries are contained in F. S. Regs., Part II. and the Staff Manual respectively. Title Pages will be prepared in manuscript.

WAR DIARY
or
~~INTELLIGENCE SUMMARY~~
(Erase heading not required.)

88th Brigade R.F.A. 19 Div

Army Form C. 2118

Vol 12

Place	Date	Hour	Summary of Events and Information	Remarks and references to Appendices
DERNACOURT	1/7/16		At 6·30am, Hd. Qr., A & B Batteries moved to a position of assembly about E.9.D.2.3 (Map 62D. N.E 1/20,000). Zero time for assault by Infantry was 7·30am	
			At 10·0am 'A' & 'B' Batteries & D/152 Battery. R.F.A. moved forward to BECOURT WOOD & were halted in the open glade at X.25.D. with bridges & bridging party with each battery	
			The Colonel with a reconnaissance officer & party from each Battery attempted to advance up SAUSAGE VALLEY but were held up by M.Gs & Barrage of 5·9" Hows across the valley, the parties suffering slight casualties in personnel & horses.	
			At 6·30pm the 34th Division ordered these Batteries to return to their wagon lines as LA BOISSELLE was still holding out; Batteries eventually left BECOURT WOOD at 8pm & returned to their wagon lines at E.9.D.2.3.	
	2/7/16 to		Batteries still at wagon lines & patrols sent forward daily to patrol routes.	
	5/7/16		D/88 Battery rejoined the Brigade from 89th Brigade on 2/7/16	
	6/7/16		B/88 Battery went into action at X21.B. & came under orders of the Right Group	
			A/88 & C/88 Batteries came into action about E.1.B. Central & were joined by D/87th Battery R.F.A. these three batteries being known as the Centre Group	
	7/7/16		The Infantry supported by the Group Artillery Fire attacked & captured LA BOISSELLE.	
	8/7/16 to 9/7/16		Fairly quiet days - ~~Enemy~~ Hostile Fire very slight.	
	10/7/16		The Infantry, supported by the Artillery fire attacked & captured CONTALMAISON. For the purpose B/88 pushed up a single gun to very close range which was of great assistance	

1875 Wt. W593/826 1,000,000 4/15 J.B.C. & A. A.D.S.S./Forms/C. 2118.

Instructions regarding War Diaries and Intelligence Summaries are contained in F. S. Regs., Part II. and the Staff Manual respectively. Title Pages will be prepared in manuscript.

WAR DIARY
or
INTELLIGENCE SUMMARY
(Erase heading not required.)

Army Form C. 2118

Place	Date	Hour	Summary of Events and Information	Remarks and references to Appendices
	11th		Fairly quiet day. Small parties of Germans seen at intervals during the day and dispersed.	
	12th		B & D/88th Batteries came out of action & came under orders of the Centre Group, D/87th returned to the 87th Brigade.	
			During the night a section of guns of A/88, C/88 & D/88 moved forward to a position about X.21.A & commenced registration of POZIERS.	
	13th		Hd-Qrs moved from BECOURT WOOD to German Dug-Out in X.21.A.	
			B/88 Battery moved up from wagon line to a position in X.21.A & commenced registration	
	14th		Batteries completed their registrations.	
	15th to 18th		Registration – wire cutting & minor operations between POZIERS & CONTALMAISON.	
	19th		Fairly quiet day. In the evening the Brigade was partially relieved by the 3rd Brigade R.F.A. 1st Australian Division at 11 pm.	
	20th		Relief completed by 9am & Brigade moved to new wagon lines in F.7.B.7.3.	
			At 2pm Brigade moved complete to new positions at S.20 B & commenced registration of their new zone. All wagon lines being at F.7.B.7.3.	
	21st		Fairly quiet day & batteries completed their registrations	
	22nd		Bombarded the "INTERMEDIATE TRENCH" & "SWITCH LINE" & the Infantry attacked.	
	23rd		Wagon Lines moved back to their old position at E.9.B. owing to the enemy shelling of F.7.B.	
	24th		Heavy shelling by the enemy in the neighbourhood of S.20 B	

Army Form C. 2118

Instructions regarding War Diaries and Intelligence Summaries are contained in F. S. Regs., Part II. and the Staff Manual respectively. Title Pages will be prepared in manuscript.

WAR DIARY
or
INTELLIGENCE SUMMARY
(Erase heading not required.)

Place	Date	Hour	Summary of Events and Information	Remarks and references to Appendices
	25/7/16		Severe Hostile shelling throughout the day.	
	26/7/16		Severe Hostile shelling, C/88 Battery moved to a new position at MAMETZ WOOD	
	27/7/16		From 5 pm to 8 pm all Batteries commenced bombarding German front line & COURCELETTE in order to create a diversion as the 13th Corps, on our right were attacking DELVILLE WOOD & LONGUEVAL.	
	28/7/16		Severe Hostile shelling	
	29/7/16		" " " B/88 Battery took a single gun forward to HIGH WOOD for the following days operations.	
	30/7/16		Batteries shelled strong points in INTERMEDIATE & SWITCH LINE & maintained fire throughout the night.	
			Night 30/31st Infantry - 54th Bde - attacked the Intermediate Line at 6.10 pm - successful on the right but no progress on left. 88th Bde had the rôle of observing hostile M.Gs & strong points. - Batteries firing without cessation from 6pm to 5am.	
	31/7/16		Very little hostile firing - very quiet day	

[illegible] for Lieut: Col: RFA
Commdg 88th Brigade RFA

1875 Wt. W593/826 1,000,000 4/15 J.B.C. & A. A.D.S.S./Forms/C. 2118.

19th Divl. Arty. No B.M./ 365/B.

34th Division.
~~34th Divisional Artillery.~~

========================

Report on Operations night 17th/18th
by
O.C. 88th F.A.Brigade.

* * * *

The Artillery programme appeared to be carried out according to programme but the enemy artillery fire was so heavy that telephone lines were repeatedly broken and lamp signalling was never effectively established between my F.O.O. with advanced battalions and O.P's.

The enemy's artillery fire was particularly heavy at the head of SAUSAGE VALLEY and in X 15 c X 16. The whole of these areas were searched continuously from 7.30p.m. to 2.30a.m. with 5.9's, high velocity guns about 5.2 and field Artillery.

From F.O.O. reports it appears that our Infantry were held up after advancing 100 yards by very heavy machine-gun fire - it is reported that at least 10 M.Guns were firing at short range.

Very heavy fire appeared to come from the neighbourhood of X 14 c 7.4.

At 12 midnight our attacking Infantry were back in their original line having had very heavy casualties, except at point 41 which we now hold. It is reported that some of our Field Guns were firing 200 yards short and into our own Infantry. It is not possible to identify the batteries firing short, but careful registration is required for such close shooting and some of the Batteries, not of 19th Divisional Artillery, firing last night, can scarcely have had time to register properly. ~~xxxxx~~ It is probable that some Observing Officers have not identified the line held by, and the objectives of, our Infantry.

Lieut. BENNET, D/88 F.O.O. reports that he was with 12 Durhams at about X 10 b 5.8 during the operation and in our front line (12 Durhams now relieved by 10/N.F.)

Previous to the Artillery lift, there was very little German Machine Gun fire and few flares sent up. Immediately the Artillery lifted Machine Gun fire became intense and many flares were sent up. Machine Gun fire chiefly from X 4 c 7.4 and about X 4 d 3.5. No-man's land was also very heavily enfiladed by Machine Gun fire from the direction of X 3 b 8.1.

Throughout the operation the enemy Artillery barrage in X 9 b X 10 a and X 10 b with 5.9, 4.2 and 77.mm. was intense.

The Artillery barrage appeared good and lifted well except for one 18-pdr. Battery which persistently fired in X 10 b 9.8.

None of our Infantry moved forward until five minutes after the Artillery lift - one Company did not move at all. When our Infantry moved the German Machine Gun fire was already intense.

The Infantry report that the trench X 4 c 6.2. - X 4 d 1.1. - 8.2. was "full of Germans".

4/186

Lieut. BENNET is of opinion that had our Infantry crept forward as close as possible under the Artillery barrage and rushed in on the lift they would have got home without very large casualties.

I am directing my Batteries to carefully re-register this afternoon the zone allotted to them in German front line for today's operation and suggest that all other batteries should do the same.

There is no doubt that the Germans are now showing green lights in their lines and that our signal is becoming valueless.

The Germans are also freely using red lights, meaning not known.

Have the General Staff any information as to German signals ? Any information would be useful but it should not be communicated to those under the rank of F.A.Brigade and Battalion Commanders.

(sgd) G.S.TOVEY Lieut. Col R.F.A.
18.7.16. Commanding 88th F.A.Brigade.

* * * *

W. P. Monkhouse

Brigadier General.
18.7.1916. Commanding R.A., 19th Division.

19th Divisional Artillery

<u>88th BRIGADE</u>

<u>ROYAL FIELD ARTILLERY</u>

<u>AUGUST 1 9 1 6</u> ::::

Instructions regarding War Diaries and Intelligence Summaries are contained in F. S. Regs., Part II. and the Staff Manual respectively. Title pages will be prepared in manuscript.

WAR DIARY or INTELLIGENCE SUMMARY.

(Erase heading not required.)

88 Bde R.F.A. Army Form C. 2118.

Vol 13

Place	Date	Hour	Summary of Events and Information	Remarks and references to Appendices
N.13.c.2.9. Trench Map 1/10000 WYTSCHAETE Edition 3.D	1/8/16		Fairly quiet day – Bursts of hostile fire at intervals during the day in front of Bde Hd-Qrs & in the neighbourhood of CATERPILLAR VALLEY.	
	2/8/16		Quiet during the day – very little hostile fire. From 9pm until 11pm the Brigade, supported by the 86th & 87th Brigades bombarded the enemy's line preparatory to an attack by the Infantry. At 10am the 112th Infantry Brigade attacked the INTERMEDIATE LINE from about S.2.D.9.5 to S.2.c.8.5 & captured about 150 yards of it.	
	3/8/16		Fairly quiet day – in the evening one Section of each Battery were relieved by a section of the 72nd Brigade R.F.A & upon relief returned to their wagon lines at E.9.D.2.3.	
	4/8/16		At 8am the relieved sections of each Battery & part of Brigade Hd-Qrs marched to BAVELINCOURT & camped there. At 10pm the remainder of the relief was completed & the command taken over by O.C 72nd Brigade R.F.A	
	5/8/16		At 10am remainder of Bde Hd-Qrs marched to BEHENCOURT where the advanced party had encamped – remaining sections of Batteries joined the advanced Sections at BAVELINCOURT	
	6/8/16		At 11.15am A/88 Battery marched to SALEUX & entrained for CASSEL. 'B' 'C', & 'D' Batteries followed at intervals & also entrained	
	7/8/16		At 8.55 Hd-Qrs entrained & arrived at CASSEL about 8pm. From there they marched	

T2134. Wt. W708–776. 500000. 4/15. Sir J. C. & S.

Instructions regarding War Diaries and Intelligence Summaries are contained in F. S. Regs., Part II. and the Staff Manual respectively. Title pages will be prepared in manuscript.

WAR DIARY
or
INTELLIGENCE SUMMARY.
(Erase heading not required.)

Army Form C. 2118.

Place	Date	Hour	Summary of Events and Information	Remarks and references to Appendices
			Contd	
			to EECKE & joined the remainder of the Brigade who were encamped there.	
	8/8/16		In the evening one Section of each Battery relieved one Section of the 150th Brigade in action	
	9/8/16		Bde Hd. Qrs relieved Hd Qrs of 150th Bde in action at N13.c 2.9 – Batteries relieved remaining sections of	
			150th Brigade & relief completed by 10 pm. C/89th Battery who relieved C/33 Battery [illegible] under	
			orders of the Brigade which is now known as the Left Group	[illegible]
			Positions in action of the Group are as follows: Hd Qrs N13.c 2.9., A/33. N15 a 9 6., B/33 N14 [illegible]	[illegible]
			C/33 N10 a 2½ 3½, D/33 N14 c 7 3½. & C/89 N10 a 3 8. Area covered by the Group [illegible] H 1 a to L 5.	[illegible]
	10/8/16		Batteries registered various points in their zone – hostile fire very feeble	[illegible]
	11/8/16		Further registrations carried out. During the evening enemy T.M. [illegible] were [illegible] active in	
			our zone but ceased upon being fired on	
	12/8/16		Enemy again active with T.Ms between 3 & 3.30 pm otherwise a quiet day	
	13/8/16		Quiet day nothing of interest to report.	
	14/8/16		Between 3 pm & 3.35 pm a heavy bombardment was made on enemy front & support trenches	
			in our zone which appeared to be very effective – Retaliation by enemy was weak	
	15/8/16		Quiet day. Between 5 pm & 5.30 pm 3 working parties were observed in C.13 A & dispersed	
	16/8/16		Trench Mortars more active than usual	

T2134. Wt. W708—776. 500090. 4/15. Sir J. C. & S.

Instructions regarding War Diaries and Intelligence Summaries are contained in F. S. Regs., Part II. and the Staff Manual respectively. Title pages will be prepared in manuscript.

WAR DIARY
or
INTELLIGENCE SUMMARY.
(Erase heading not required.)

Army Form C. 2118.

Place	Date	Hour	Summary of Events and Information	Remarks and references to Appendices
	17/8/16		Quiet day. Trench Mortar located at N.18.a.5½.1½. & 6 direct hits obtained on it.	
	18/8/16		" " Good deal of new work observed in enemy lines about N.18.B.6.2½. to N.18.B.2.2½.	
	19/8/16		Minor operation carried out in conjunction with T.Ms & 6" Hows to destroy (a) Suspected mine shaft at N24.A.6.8, (b) Trench Mortar located at N.24.a.5½.6½, (c) Machine Gun located at N.24.A.7.8½. Operation appeared to be effective & much timber etc was thrown up.	
	20/8/16		Quiet day nothing to report	
	21/8/16		" " " "	
	22/8/16		" " Enemy barricade across SUNKEN ROAD has been greatly strengthened & heightened & a good deal of work done to trenches in N.18.c & B.	
	23/8/16		Quiet day nothing to report	
	24/8/16		" D/88 withdrawn from the group & taken over by 89th Brigade who are known as Howitzer Group.	
	25/8/16		Enemy fairly active with 4.2s in neighbourhood of VIERSTRAAT. Suspected Blockhouse is being built in enemy lines about N18.B.1½.1½. & a M.G. located at N.18.B.2.7.	
	26/8/16		Quiet day nothing to report.	
	27/8/16		Enemy Anti-Aircraft Gun located at O.20.c., fired at it but range too long to be effective.	
	28/8/16		Hostile Minenwerfer & T.Ms very active against our front line from 1.40pm to 3.30pm	

T2134. Wt. W708–776. 50(090. 4/15. Sir J. C. & S.

WAR DIARY
or
INTELLIGENCE SUMMARY.
(Erase heading not required.)

Army Form C. 2118.

Instructions regarding War Diaries and Intelligence Summaries are contained in F. S. Regs., Part II. and the Staff Manual respectively. Title pages will be prepared in manuscript.

Place	Date	Hour	Summary of Events and Information	Remarks and references to Appendices
	29/3/16		Minor offensive operation carried out from 2-30 pm to 4-30 pm against enemy line N.18.a.2.5½ - N.18.D.1½.7 - N.18.D.9¾.9¼. which appeared effective but retaliation by enemy was poor.	
	30/3/16		No firing at all took place on either side - Raining throughout the day	
	31/3/16		A/88 Battery had to move to a position at N.15.B.2.7 owing to their old position being badly flooded with recent rains.	

[illegible] for
[illegible] Cm 88th F.A. Bde.

T2134. Wt. W708–776. 500000. 4/15. Sir J. C. & S.

Instructions regarding War Diaries and Intelligence Summaries are contained in F. S. Regs., Part II. and the Staff Manual respectively. Title pages will be prepared in manuscript.

WAR DIARY
or
INTELLIGENCE SUMMARY.
(*Erase heading not required.*)

Army Form C. 2118.

88 Bde R F A
Vol 14

Place	Date	Hour	Summary of Events and Information	Remarks and references to Appendices
	1/9/16		Enemy active against battery position in N.25.a between 11am & 3pm with 4.2s.	Refer. Trench Map 1/10,000. WYTSCHAETE Edition 3 a
	2/9/16		Quiet day nothing to report.	
	3/9/16		" " light bad for observation throughout the day.	
	4/9/16		" " a lot of work has been done by the enemy to strong point at N.24.&.0.3½	
	5/9/16		Quiet during day. In the evening Batteries shelled communication trenches in N.18.D & O.13.c. in view of suspected German relief.	
	6/9/16		A new commn. trench is being dug in No Mans Land joining enemy front line at N.18.D.2½.3 & N.18.D.2½.4½.	
			In the evening 1 section of each battery were relieved by a section of the 9th Canadian Artillery Brigade	
	7/9/16		Bde. Hd. Qrs were relieved at 12 noon & remaining sections of batteries in the evening after dark, command of the group being taken over by O.C. 9th Canadian Artillery Brigade at 6 pm.	
			Upon relief the Brigade marched by Batteries to billets at R.32.B.	Ref Sheet 27
	8/9/16		The 18 Pdr Batteries of the Brigade re-organized & formed into 6 gun Batteries. The Brigade now consists of 3-18 Pdr. Batteries (A.B & C Batteries) & 1. 4.5 Howitzer Battery (D/88).	
			In the evening 1 section of each battery relieved 1 section of the 104th Brigade R.F.A. 23rd Div. Arty in action guns in each case being exchanged	Ref. Sheet 36
	9/9/16		Remainder of the relief completed. New zone taken over is from C.11.c.4½.8½ to C.4.a.8.2	

T2134. Wt. W708—776. 500000. 4/15. Sir J. C. & S.

Instructions regarding War Diaries and Intelligence Summaries are contained in F. S. Regs., Part II. and the Staff Manual respectively. Title pages will be prepared in manuscript.

WAR DIARY
or
INTELLIGENCE SUMMARY.
(Erase heading not required.)

Army Form C. 2118.

Place	Date	Hour	Summary of Events and Information	Remarks and references to Appendices
	9/9/16		Positions in action of H.Q. Gr[illegible] & Batteries are as follows: H.Q. [illegible] B.12 central, A/88 [illegible]	[illegible] Sheet 36
			4 guns C.13.D.0.4., B/88 C.2A.5.5., C/98 C.14.C.7.9, D/88 C.1.D.15	
	10/9/16		Batteries commenced registration in their new zones.	
	11/9/16		Further registration carried out.	
	12/9/16		" " " "	
	13/9/16		Enemy wire cut in neighbourhood of C.4.A.7.4½ & C.4A.7.5½ also between C.4.D.15.47. & C.4.D.25.35. with a view to a raid by the 58th Infantry Brigade.	
	14/9/16		Wire cutting operation of previous day continued & gaps already cut were enlarged.	
	15/9/16		Batteries registered selected points for supporting the raid. At 9 pm the raiding party went out but were forced to return on account of rifle & machine gun fire as the enemy were fully prepared for them.	
	16/9/16		Between 10am & noon enemy Trench Mortars were very active against Sectors 111 – 110 [illegible]	
	17/9/16		Quiet day. In the evening Batteries in conjunction with the 49th Heavy Artillery Group fired salvoes at 7.30 pm, 9 pm, 10.10 pm & 12.15 am on selected objectives in German lines.	
	18/9/16		Very quiet day – no activity on either side	
	19/9/16		Quiet Day – a few registrations carried out by batteries	

Army Form C. 2118.

Instructions regarding War Diaries and Intelligence Summaries are contained in F. S. Regs., Part II. and the Staff Manual respectively. Title pages will be prepared in manuscript.

WAR DIARY
or
INTELLIGENCE SUMMARY.

(Erase heading not required.)

Place	Date	Hour	Summary of Events and Information	Remarks and references to Appendices
	20/9/16		Quiet on our front. At 12.30 pm there was a bombardment by T.Ms to the north of our zone which lasted about ½ an hour.	Reference Sheet 36
	21/9/16		Quiet day nothing to report	
	22/9/16		Quiet day. At 12.40 pm a German Balloon was brought down on our front. The wire cut a few days ago has been filled in by enemy & parapet opposite Point 100 has been heavily wired	
	23/9/16		Quiet day. More wire has been thrown into the gap at Point 100.	
	24/9/16		" "	
	25/9/16		" "	
	26/9/16		Registration of Special Objectives preparatory to raid by the Infantry	
	27/9/16		" " " " continued	
	28/9/16		Quiet day – a few T.Ms active against C.10.B. between 4.30 & 5 pm	
	29/9/16		" "	
	30/9/16		" " registration checked. At 10 pm the Infantry Raiding Party went out but raid did not prove a success.	

[illegible signature]
LIEUT. R.F.A.
ADJUTANT 88th BRIGADE R.F.A.

T2134. Wt. W708–776. 500000. 4/15. Sir J. C. & S.

Instructions regarding War Diaries and Intelligence Summaries are contained in F. S. Regs., Part II. and the Staff Manual respectively. Title pages will be prepared in manuscript.

WAR DIARY
or
INTELLIGENCE SUMMARY.
(Erase heading not required.)

88th RFA Brigade

Army Form C. 2118.

VOL 15

Place	Date	Hour	Summary of Events and Information	Remarks and references to Appendices
	1/10/16		From 9am to 2pm the enemy continuously shelled (c) 13.D.6.2 & vicinity. In the evening 1 Section of each battery were relieved by 1 Section of the 22nd Brigade R.F.A.	Ref: Map 1/10,000 PLOEGSTEERT
	2/10/16		Remaining Sections of each Battery relieved & Hd Qrs & the Brigade marched to rest billets at GODESWARVELDE.	
	3/10/16		Ordinary Brigade Routine	
	4/10/16		" " "	
	5/10/16		" " "	
	6/10/16		Commencing at 5.15am the Brigade entrained at GODESWARDELDE and detrained at CANDAS & marched to VAUCHELLES where temporary billets were taken.	
	7/10/16		Brigade marched to new wagon lines near ~~St~~ St LEGER	
	8/10/16		Bde Hd Qrs moved to position in action at K.17.D.6.7½ & digging parties from each battery commenced preparing new battle positions.	Ref Map 1/20,000 HEBUTERNE
	9/10/16		Work on new positions continued	
	10/10/16		" " "	
	11/10/16		Batteries moved up to positions in action about K.14.B & D & preliminary registration were carried out	

T2134. Wt. W708-776. 500000. 4/15. Sir J. C. & S.

Army Form C. 2118.

Instructions regarding War Diaries and Intelligence Summaries are contained in F. S. Regs., Part II. and the Staff Manual respectively. Title pages will be prepared in manuscript.

WAR DIARY
or
INTELLIGENCE SUMMARY.
(*Erase heading not required.*)

Place	Date	Hour	Summary of Events and Information	Remarks and references to Appendices
	12/10/16		Wire cutting operations commenced + 3 lanes each about 24 yards wide were cut in enemy's wire at K.17.B.7½.9., K.17.B.9½.5. + K.18.A.1.3.	Ref. 1/20,000 HEBUTERNE Map
	13/10/16		Work on Battle Positions continued during the day. From 8.30 to 10.30 pm 'A' + 'B' Batteries heavily shelled the trench running from L.13.D.0.5 to L.18.D.5.7. + enemy front line in conjunction with a "noise demonstration" made by the Infantry.	
	14/10/16		Registration of selected objectives carried out with a view to an advance being made by the Infantry.	
	15/10/16		Further wire cutting done by "A" Battery about K.17.B.0.7. with good results.	
	16/10/16		Quiet Day. - In the evening the Brigade zone was taken over by the 170th Brigade R.F.A. + the Brigade returned to its wagon lines.	
	17/10/16		At 8am the Brigade marched to new area + wagon lines were taken up between ALBERT + AUVELY (W.22A.3.9.). During the night Batteries moved up into action at	
	18/10/16		Brigade Hd. Qrs moved to forward area + established themselves at R.32.B.2½.2½. + registration of zone completed.	
	19/10/16		New zone taken over + registered.	

T2134. Wt. W708–776. 500000. 4/15. Sir J. C. & S.

Instructions regarding War Diaries and Intelligence Summaries are contained in F. S. Regs., Part II. and the Staff Manual respectively. Title pages will be prepared in manuscript.

WAR DIARY
or
INTELLIGENCE SUMMARY.
(Erase heading not required.)

Army Form C. 2118.

Place	Date	Hour	Summary of Events and Information	Remarks and references to Appendices
	20/10/16		At 6am bombardment of enemy front line carried out & other selected spots in zone & some points kept under intermittent fire throughout the night.	
	21/10/16		Programme of previous day repeated. Infantry attacked & Regina Trench was taken together with about 1100 prisoners	
	22/10/16		Enemy counter-attacked but were repulsed & about 42 prisoners were taken by us	
	23rd to 31st		Enemy front line, selected points in rear, & approaches to GRANDCOURT kept under intermittent fire throughout the day & night.	

F. Army [illegible]

T2134. Wt. W708–776. 500000. 4/15. Sir J. C. & S.

Instructions regarding War Diaries and Intelligence Summaries are contained in F. S. Regs., Part II. and the Staff Manual respectively. Title Pages will be prepared in manuscript.

WAR DIARY
or
INTELLIGENCE SUMMARY
(Erase heading not required.)

Army Form C. 2118.

88th Brigade R.F.A.
Vol 12

Place	Date	Hour	Summary of Events and Information	Remarks and references to Appendices
	1/II/16		Enemy defences, wire & strong points were kept under intermittent bursts of fire throughout the night.	
	2/II/16		A quiet day, enemy artillery showing no activity. Night firing was carried out as for last night and also bridges over the ANCRE were kept under fire.	
	3/II/16.		Much activity by enemy aeroplanes throughout the day which was followed by increased artillery fire about MOUQUET FARM and slight shelling of NAB VALLEY.	
	4/II/16 } 5/II/16 }		No action to report during day; enemy defences, dug-outs and bridges over the ANCRE in Brigade zone were kept under fire throughout the night.	
	6/II/16		" " " " " " " "	
	7/II/16		Heavy enemy shelling of LUCKY WAY and STUFF TRENCH. Our artillery retaliated until the shelling ceased.	
	8/II/16		Throughout the day and night we intermittently shelled Bridges over the ANCRE in the Brigade zone.	
	9/II/16		There was much aerial activity on both sides chiefly during the afternoon. Enemy shelled rear areas considerably. At about 10.30 "Gas Alert" was received but it was ~~found~~ afterwards ascertained that the enemy was shelling with Gas shell; the gas did not reach the vicinity of the Brigade and "Alert" was taken off.	
	10/II/16		At 5.30 a.m. we put on an intense bombardment ~~was~~ which was very effective the only retaliation being directed against SCHWABEN and that neighbourhood. Night firing was carried out over ~~Brigades~~ bridges over the ANCRE as per programme.	
	11/II/16		We again took part in the early morning bombardment with half the guns of the Brigade. During the night, about 11 p.m. several enemy aeroplanes were heard proceeding in the direction of ALBERT and it was afterwards found out that bombs had been dropped in that neighbourhood. This was the commencement of several similar expeditions which followed during the next few nights.	
	12/II/16		Enemy defences were kept under continuous fire throughout the day; the enemy shelled the locality of MOUQUET FARM with 5.9". Night firing on enemy dug-outs, bridges over the ANCRE .	
	13/II/16		At 5.45 a.m. the brigade opened their Barrage as per Battle Programme, when the infantry advanced under it to the enemy line where they met with little opposition, the enemy being unprepared owing to our having bombarded on the previous mornings. Infantry took their objectives and many prisoners with slight lossess to themselves. The enemy's counter-barrage was feeble and slow in being put on. The HANSA LINE was captured.	
	14/II/16		At 6.15 a.m. the Brigade opened their Barrage as per Battle Programme when the infantry made	

Instructions regarding War Diaries and Intelligence Summaries are contained in F. S. Regs., Part II. and the Staff Manual respectively. Title Pages will be prepared in manuscript.

WAR DIARY
or
INTELLIGENCE SUMMARY

(Erase heading not required.)

Army Form C. 2118.

Place	Date	Hour	Summary of Events and Information	Remarks and references to Appendices
			large bombind raids and took up an advanced line, and made some prisoners. Exits to GRANDCOURT were shelled during the night with 18-pdrs and 4.5" Hows:	
	15/II/16		Much enemy aerial activity throughout the afternoon, and again he made night flights dropping bombs in rear area.	
	16/II/16		Afternoon was very clear for visibility and many parties of enemy were seen by aeroplane observers whose calls to engage these targets were answered; one party were routed being seen to run into dug-outs. Enemy dug-outs, and defences were kept under fire all night, but only desultorily.	
	17/II/16		Bridges over the ANCRE in Brigade Zone where shelled desultorily during the day. "S.O.S." signal was received on the enemy opening heavy fire on our trenches, and "S.O.S." barrage was put on at Slow rate of fire until the shelling ceased. Night firing was carried out throughtout the night.	
	18/II/16		At zero, Batteries opened their Barrage as per Battle Programme and Infantry attacked in conjunction with Division on our right and left. It was reported by F.O.O. that certain parts of our objectives had been taken, but that others were held up. GRANDCOURT was reported captured but at the conclusion of operations, the position was very obscure, and the exact location of our line was doubtful necessitating great care in our firing.	
	19/II/16) 20/II/16(21/II/16		Very quiet days, only desultory shelling taking place. On 20th we took over part of 17th D.A. Zone. Desultory shelling of bridges over the River ANCRE. At 5 p.m. "S.O.S." signals were received and fire was opened on WRETCHED WAY, bridges over thexANCRE and roads, until the situation was clear. These targets were kept under fire throughout the night.	
	22/II/16		We shelled RIVER TRENCH, PUISIEUX TRENCH, and MIRAUMONT ALLEY during the day, and night. Also bursts of fire on O.G.I., and O.G.2.	
	23/II/16) to) 28/II/16)		Deliberate shelling of enemy defences and approaches. Orders were received to salve all empty shell cases and stores lying in Brigade Area and this work was carried out, all empty cases being returned and many stores being collected together.	
	28/II/16		During the afternoon and through the evening till after midnight an intense Gas shell bombardment was carried out on Cross Roads and other selected points. toether with 18pdr fire.	
	29/II/16		At 6 p.m. in response to infantry's call for retaliation fire was opened on various points till hostile shelling ceased,	
	30/II/16		Fire was opened on "S.O.S." lines at 5.35 a.m. in compliance with orders of 19th D.A. After firing for nearly half an hour, the situation was reported all quiet and fire was stopped.	

[signature] COLONEL, R.F.A.
COMMDG. 89th BRIGADE R.F.A.

2449 Wt. W14957/M90 750,000 1/16 J.B.C. & A. Forms/C.2118/12.

Instructions regarding War Diaries and Intelligence Summaries are contained in F. S. Regs., Part II. and the Staff Manual respectively. Title Pages will be prepared in manuscript.

WAR DIARY
or
INTELLIGENCE SUMMARY
(Erase heading not required.)

Army Form C. 2118.

88 Bde R F A

Vol 17

Place	Date	Hour	Summary of Events and Information	Remarks and references to Appendices
	I/I2/I6		Quiet day. Nothing to report.	
	2/I2/I6		Quiet day. " " "	
	3/I2/I6		" " . At noon the zone of 87th Bde. R.F.A. was taken over in addition to ~~xxx~~ our own.	
	4/I2/I6		Brigade came out of actions and marched to wagon lines, ammunition having been handed over to IIth D.A.	
	5/I2/I6		Ordinary parades carried out and cleaning up generally.	
	6/I2/I6		At 9 a.m. the Brigade left wagon lines and marched via BOUZANCOURT - HEDAUVILLE - VARENNES, - LEALVILLERS - RAINCHEVAL - MARIEUX - SARTON to AMPLIER where billets were taken.	
	7/I2/I6		March resumed and Brigade arrived at OUTREBOIS and took up billets in that neighbourhood.	
	8/I2/I6		Ordinary Brigade routine.	
	9/I2/I6		Commencement of general scheme for the improvement of billeting area including repairs to billets, making better accomodation, building cook-houses, horse-standings, incinerators etc. Cleaning up generally in harness, vehicles etc.	
	IO/I2/I6)			
	II/I2/I6)			
	I2/I2/I6)		" " " " " " " " "	
	I3/I2/I6)			
	I4/I2/I6)			
	I5/I2/I6)			
	I6/I2/I6)			
	I7/I2/I6)			
	I8/I2/I6		Brigade parade and inspection by V Corps Commander.	
	I9/I2/I6)			
	20/I2/I6)			
	2I/I2/I6)			
	22/I2/I6)		Work as above, resumed.	
	23/I2/I6)			
	24/I2/I6)			
	25/I2/I6)			
	26/I2/I6)			
	27/I2/I6)			
	28/I2/I6)			
	29/I2/I6)			

2449 Wt. W14957/M90 750,000 1/16 J.B.C. & A. Forms/C.2118/12.

Instructions regarding War Diaries and Intelligence Summaries are contained in F. S. Regs., Part II. and the Staff Manual respectively. Title Pages will be prepared in manuscript.

WAR DIARY
or
INTELLIGENCE SUMMARY
(Erase heading not required.)

Army Form C. 2118.

Place	Date	Hour	Summary of Events and Information	Remarks and references to Appendices
	30/12/16		Orders received that Brigade would march to AUTHIEULE on I/I/17 and preparations made accordingly.	
	31/12/16		Inspection of Brigade in Field Service Marching Order by the Brigade Commander.	

Major, R.F.A.
Commanding 83th Brigade, R.F.A.

2449 Wt. W14957/M90 750,000 1/16 J.B.C. & A. Forms/C.2118/12.

Army Form C. 2118.

Instructions regarding War Diaries and Intelligence Summaries are contained in F. S. Regs., Part II. and the Staff Manual respectively. Title Pages will be prepared in manuscript.

WAR DIARY
or
INTELLIGENCE SUMMARY

(Erase heading not required.)

Place	Date	Hour	Summary of Events and Information	Remarks and references to Appendices
	1/I/17		Brigade marched from OUTREBOIS to AUTHIELE via OCCOCHES - HEM - and took up billets for the night.	LENS II 1/100000
	2/I/17		Marched from AUTHIELE via AMPLIER,-SARTON to THIEVRES and established wagon lines here. Guns, gun line personnel etc continued the march via AUTHIE, BUS and COURCELLES and took up positions in action as follows:- H.Q. at COURCELLES - A/88 at K.26.D.Central - B/88 at K.27.A.2.2 - C/88 at K.21.C.3.0 - D/88 at K.20.D.0.8. Teams returned to wagon lines at THIEVRES. The Brigade was attached to and came under the orders of the C.R.A. 3rd Division on this date.	HEBUTERNE 1/10000
	3/I/17		Registration commenced of points in Zones and of night lines.	"
	4/I/17		" continued.	"
	5/I/17		" "	"
	6/I/17		" "	"
	7/I/17		" "	"
	8/I/17		" "	"
	9/I/17		Bombardment of WHITE TRENCH, WALTER TRENCH, STAR ALLEY etc for 48 hours commenced at 8 a.m. in accordance with operation instructions from 3rd D.A. in connection with an assault by 7th Divn. on "Z" day, to-day being "X" day. Intense fire was kept up for periods:- 1.20 p.m. to 1.30 p.m., and 4.50 p.m. to 5 p.m. Hostile reply to this bombardment was weak. Continued throught the night.	"
	10/I/17		The bombardment was continued with intense periods at 8 a.m. to 8.10 a.m., 5.30 p.m. to 5.40 p.m. Again to-day the enemy's reply to the bombardment was feeble. The bombardment was carried on during the night. This was "Y" day.	"
	11/I/17		To-day was "Z" day and zero hour was 6.50 A.M. At - 3 Mins. all batteries (except D/88) opened out their barrage and fired on objectives as detailed in 3rd D.A. Opeation Order.	"
	12/I/17.		During the day this bombardedment was gradually dimished and only normal fire was carried out on such objectives as movement seen.	
	13/I/17.		Ordinary firing carried during the day and night on selected objectives and on movement seen during the day.	"
	14/I/17.		" " " " " " " " "	"
	15/I/17.		Batteries moved into new positions relieving the following units of 31st D.A.:- "A"/88 relieved A/165 at K.14.D.2.0 - B/88 relieved B/165 at K.14.C.2.1 - C/88 relieved C/165 at K.13.A.6.6 D/88 relieved D/165 at J.6.B.9.8. - H.Q./88 relieved H.Q./165 at THE QUARRIES, SAILLY-AU-BOIS. The relief of one section of each batterywas completed by 8 a.m. and the remainder at 4 p.m.	"
	16/I/17		Bde: H.Q. moved and established at BAYENCOURT. Registration of new zone continued by Batteries. "A"/86 in action at K.2.A.65.35 - "C"/86 in action at K.13.A.63.35 - "D"/86 in action at K.2.C.23.33 all came under the orders of this Bde: and together with batteries 88th Bde: formed the LEFT GROUP, 19th D.A. During night roads & tracks in enemy's lines kept under intermittent fire.	"

2449 Wt. W14957/M90 750,000 1/16 J.B.C. & A. Forms/C.2118/12.

Army Form C. 2118.

Instructions regarding War Diaries and Intelligence Summaries are contained in F. S. Regs., Part II. and the Staff Manual respectively. Title Pages will be prepared in manuscript.

WAR DIARY
or
INTELLIGENCE SUMMARY

(Erase heading not required.)

Place	Date	Hour	Summary of Events and Information	Remarks and references to Appendices
	17/I/17		Registration of new zone continued. "C"/87 Battery joined the LEFT GROUP to-day, it being in action at K.20.B.I2.60. During the day the enemy's front line, communication trenches and selected objectives were kept under desultory fire, and during he night roads and tracks were intermittently kept under fire.	HEBUTERNE I/IO,000
	18/I/17		" " " " " " " "	
	19/I/17		" " " " " " " "	
	20/I/17		" " " " " " " "	
	21/I/17		" " " " " " " "	
	22/I/17		" " " " " " " "	
	23/I/17		" " " " " " " "	
	24/I/17		Owing to re-organization of Divisional Artillery one section of "C"/86 Battery was transferred to "D"/88 battery making it a 6- 4.5"How: Battery; the other section of "C"/86 going to "D"/87.	
	25/I/17) 26/I/17)		The usual firing on enemy front line, CT's and selected objectives was carried out during the day and on roads and tracks etc during the night, on both these days.	
	27/I/17		In addition to the usual daily firing the fire of the Group was directed against L.I.C.O.2., L.I.D.6.6., L.I3.C.5.4.,- L.I3.D.8.3.	
	28/I/16		The zone of "C"/86 Battery was taken over by "D"/88, and "D"/88 had now 4 Hows; in action in K.I3.A.63.35 and 2 Hows: at K.I.A.O.8. The usual firing was carried out.	
	29/I/17.		The usual firing programme of the Group was carried out.	
	30/I/17		In addition to the usual daily firing the fire of all the Group was directed against K.5.C.5.0 - K.5.C.3.3., K.II.B.I.6., K.5.D.7.O., K.5.B.4.O., K.II.D.8.3 - K.I2.C.5.4., K.I7.B.9.7 - K.I8.A.5.4., K.I2.A.8.7,- K.I2.B.I.8 - K.I2.B.2.4., L.7.C.2.I., E.30.D.9.5., K.I2.B.O.7., K.I2.B.3.5., K.I2.D.42.78 at frequent intervals throughout the day. Hostile artillery was normal.	
	31/I/17.		The usual firing took place and in addition the group bombarded K.I2.D.4.8., points in ROSIGNOL WOOD, K.5.D.8.7., and other points for two minutes at 4 p.m.	

[signature]
Lieut: Col: R.F.A.
Commanding 88th Brigade, R.F.A.

2449 Wt. W14957/M90 750,000 1/16 J.B.C. & A. Forms/C.2118/12.

Army Form C. 2118.

88 Bde RFA Vol 19

Instructions regarding War Diaries and Intelligence Summaries are contained in F. S. Regs., Part II. and the Staff Manual respectively. Title Pages will be prepared in manuscript.

WAR DIARY
or
INTELLIGENCE SUMMARY
(Erase heading not required.)

Place	Date	Hour	Summary of Events and Information	Remarks and references to Appendices
	1/2/17		Ordinary group firing carried out during the day on selected objectives and movement seen. Much movement was seen on road from PIGEON WOOD to ESSARTS during morning and road was at once engaged. During night, roads and tracks etc were intermittently shelled.	HEBUTERNE I/10,000 and 57D N.E I/20,000.
	2/2/17.		Usual firing took place during day on selected objectives in the Group Zone combined with concentrated bursts of fire on selected Group targets. Night firing on roads and tracks known to be used by the enemy.	
	3/2/17.) 4/2/17.) 5/2/17.) 6/2/17.) 7/2/17.) 8/2/17.)		" " " " "	
	9/2/17.		During the morning, the "S.O.S." Barrage and rapid concentration of Group fire was tested and I4 targets engaged. At 7.40 pm the "S.O.S." Barrage was put on by order of I9th D.A. in response to heavy enemy artillery fire which was afterwards found not to be on our zone, when barrage was taken off.	
	I0/2/I7.		Ordinary fire of the Group carried out and in addition the Barrage ordered for an operation on night II/I2th was rehearsed at II.0 am and 8.30 pm. Night firing on roads and tracks and selected points in the Group Zone.	
	II/2/I7.		Ditto. With rehearsal of rapid programme at 3.0 pm. Fire was concentrated on Group targets during the morning. Zero hour for raid was II.I5 pm. At Zero - I8 secs the raid barrage was put on as ordered and continued until Zero + I Hour. Enemy retaliation was slight in our zone.	
	I2/2/I7.		Ordinary Group fire was carried out during the day on selected points, i.e. ROSIGNOL WOOD, RAILWAY TERMINUS ROSIGNOL, FLIGHT TRENCH etc. Hostile artillery fairly active. Throughout the night desultory fire was kept up on roads and tracks & selected onjectives. Fire was concentrated on Group Targets during the evening.	
	I3/2/I7.) I4/2/I7.) I5/2/I7.)		Ordinary firing on selected objectives during day and on roads and tracks in rear of the enemy lines during the night. Enemy artillery rather active.	
	I6/2/I7.		In addition to usual firing, fire was concentrated at I0-30 pm and II.30 pm for 2 mins at each period on a working party with covering party, who were reported working hard during the evening.	

Army Form C. 2118.

WAR DIARY
or
INTELLIGENCE SUMMARY
(Erase heading not required.)

Instructions regarding War Diaries and Intelligence Summaries are contained in F. S. Regs., Part II. and the Staff Manual respectively. Title Pages will be prepared in manuscript.

Place	Date	Hour	Summary of Events and Information	Remarks and references to Appendices
	17/2/17.		Ordinary group firing on selected points during the day and concentrated fire on "Group Targets" at intervals during the afternoon and evening. Usual night firing.	
	18/2/17.		Quiet day with usual firing. "A"/86 and "D"/86 Batteries moved to new position as per orders of 19th D.A. and came out of the LEFT GROUP. Consequent on this, re-allotment of zones and necessary alteration to "S.O.S." lines carried out. Usual night firing.	
	19/2/17.		Daily firing programme on selected points and usual night firing carried out.	
	20/2/17.		" " " "	
	20/2/17.		" " . From 6.50 pm to 7.15 pm the enemy heavily shelled vicinity of battery position at K.14.C.25.13 with gas shells.	
	21/2/17.		Quiet day, usual firing taking place.	
	22/2/17.		" " " "	
	23/2/17.		" " " "	
	24/2/17.		" " " ". During the night one Section of each Battery was withdrawn from action being relieved by a section of corresponding batteries 165th Brigade R.F.A. in accordance with orders.	
	25/2/17.		During the afternoon orders received for batteries to complete relief immediately owing to enemy retiring on our front and move up to new positions in action as follows:- A/88 at K.15.A.0.2., B/88 at K.15.C.2.9., C/88 at K.15.D.5½.6½., D/88 at K.15.B.8½.4½. H.Q. established at SAILLY-AU-BOIS. C/87 battery left the Group.	
	26/2/17.		Registration in L.7, 8 & 9 carried out on orders from 19th D.A. during afternoon with a view to advance being made by 57th Infantry Brigade. ~~xxxxxxxx~~ Throughout the night intermittent fire was directed against ESSARTS - BUCQUOY Road and points in L.I.	
	27/2/17.		At 9.30 am enemy reported retiring along ULHENFELD GRABEN towards FORK WOOD and the Brigade brought fire to bear on this neighbourhood. On belief that the Germans would counter-attack, S.O.S. Barrage was put on at 4.50 pm but on the infantry reporting that it was not required, was taken off about 5.15 p.m. Night lines were tested at 7 pm. Night firing carried out in K.12.B & L.7.a.	
	28/2/17.		Registration carried out on Eastern corner of ROSIGNOL WOOD.	

W Forey [signature]

Lieut: Col: R.F.A.
Commanding 88th Brigade, R.F.A.

2449 Wt. W14957/M90 750,000 1/16 J.B.C. & A. Forms/C.2118/12.

Instructions regarding War Diaries and Intelligence Summaries are contained in F. S. Regs., Part II. and the Staff Manual respectively. Title Pages will be prepared in manuscript.

WAR DIARY
or
INTELLIGENCE SUMMARY

(Erase heading not required.)

Army Form C. 2118.

88 Bde RFA
Vol 20

Place	Date	Hour	Summary of Events and Information	Remarks and references to Appendices
	MARCH	Ist	Registration carried out on various points. At 3.40 p.m. ROSSINGNOL WOOD was bombarded in accordance with I9th D.A. orders. Hostile artillery was quiet during the day.	HEBUTERNE I/IO,000
	"	2nd	From I2 midnight to 2 a.m. programme arranged in support of attack by 58th Infantry Brigade carried out. During the day following targets were engaged:- K.I2.D.5.8., M.G. at K.I2.D.3.9., Snipers Post at K.I2.A.9. Enemy artillery fairly active during the day. Many fires were seen burning in ROSSIGNOL WOOD presumably dug-outs or dumps. ROSSIGNOL WOOD was evacuated by the enemy and occupied by our infantry.	
	"	3rd	From 3.20 p.m. to 5.30 p.m. BIEZ WOOD was searched and swept by out fire. Enemy artillery fire was normal. During the afternoon I Section of "A"/88 and "B"/88 each moved up into advanced positions at K.23.A.2.3 and K.23.A.2.7. respectively and were in position by 5 p.m.	
	"	4th	Registration carried out by advanced sections of "A"/88 and "B"/88. BUCQUOY and L.I.D.2½.I were engaged during the day. Hostile artillery and A.A. guns were active. BIEZ WOOD was reported evacuated by the enemy during the morning but our infantry could not enter it to confirm this on account of our own fire.	
	"	5th	"A"/88 and "D"/88 each took over three guns from "A"/59 and "D"/59 respectively in advanced positions at L.I3.C.7.7 and L.I3.D.2.4 and during the day they each took up three guns from their present positions to these advanced positions. The remaining three guns of each battery were handed over to "A"/59 and "D"/59. There was no action during the day and enemy artillery was quiet. Enemy reported in L.2.A & B., and L.3.A. Point L.2.D.3.3. was kept under intermittent fire throughout the night.	
	"	6th	Registration for wire-cutting carried out and wire-utting was carried out between L.2.D.4.O - L.2.D.4.IO and at about L.3.C.I5.05 which was not satisfactory owing to unsteadiness of gun platforms but IO yards gap believed cut at L.3.C.I5.05. Much aerial activity by both sides during the day. Enemy artillery quiet.	
	"	7th	Registration for continuance of wire-cutting carried out and wire-cutting done between L.2.D.3.5 - L.2.D.8½.8 and again on L.3.C.I5.05 - visibility was too poor to ascertain results. Reported that enemy M.Gs were active at F.26.D.7.I., F.26.D.6.2½ and L.2.B.O.9½ which were engaged by 4.5" Hows: During the night L.28.A.8.6., L.23.C.3.I., F.26.D.6.I., F.26.D.O.O were kept under intermittent fire.	
	"	8th	Wire was again attacked at about L.8.C.I5.05 and ABLAINZEVILLE was shelled by 4.5" Hows: From 4.IO pm to 4.30 pm on orders from I9th D.A. the Brigade barraged from L.2.D.8.3 - L.9.B..8 with I8-prs and from L.3.C.O.5 - L.3.C.3.3 with 4.5" Hows: in conjunction with Infantry attack which was unsuccessful. We made 5 prisoners. Enemy artillery was quiet until this operation when in response to rocket signals he barraged our front posts and shelled ROSSIGNOL WOOD.	

2449 Wt. W14957/M90 750,000 1/16 J.B.C. & A. Forms/C.2118/12.

Instructions regarding War Diaries and Intelligence Summaries are contained in F. S. Regs., Part II. and the Staff Manual respectively. Title Pages will be prepared in manuscript.

WAR DIARY
or
INTELLIGENCE SUMMARY

(Erase heading not required.)

Army Form C. 2118.

Place	Date	Hour	Summary of Events and Information	Remarks and references to Appendices
	MARCH	9th	Brigade was relieved by 59th Bde. R.F.A. batteries 88th Bde. being relieved by corresponding Batteries 59th Bde. "A"/59 and "D"/59 took over the guns of "A"/88 and "D"/88 respectively. Batteries withdrawn to wagon lines but Bde. H.Q. maintained at SAILLY-AU- BOIS.	HEBUTERN E I/IO,000
	"	IOth	Ordinary Brigade Routine and preparations made to move on IIth by road to 2nd Army Area as per orders. Billeting parties sent in advance to-day.	
	"	IIth	The Brigade marched from Wagon Lines via AUTHIE, THIEVRES, SARTON, DOULLENS to OCCCCHES and HEM and billets taken for the night.	LENS II I/IOO,000
	"	I2th	March resumed via OUTREBOIS, BARLY, BONNIERES, FORTEL & VACQUERIE to BOUBERS-SUR-CANCHE and billets taken.	
	"	I3th	March resumed via CONCHY, E inBLANGERVAL, LINZEUX, BEAUVOIS, BERNICOURT, FLEURY and ANVIN to BERGUENEUSE and billets taken.	
	"	I4th	Ordinary Brigade Routine and cleaning up.	
	"	I5th	March again resumed via WESTERHEM - RELY to QUERNES and WITTERESSE and billets taken.	HAZEBROUCK I/IOO,000
	"	I6th	Ordinary Brigade Routine and cleaning up.	
	"	I7th	March again resumed via AIRE, & STEENBECQUE to MORBECQUES and billets taken.	
	"	I8th	March resumed via HAZEBROUCK, BOURRE - STRAZEELE to VIEUX BERGUIN and billets taken.	
	"	I9th	March resumed via STRAZEELE - CAESTRE - CASSEL to NOORPEENE and OEHTZEELE and billets taken.	
	"	20th	March resumed via Route N.W. of FORET D'EPERLECQUES to 2nd Army Training Area near POLINCOVE and billets taken in POLINCOVE.	
	"	2Ist to 29th	Training carried out. Cleaning up generally including painting of vehicles and re-fitting.	
	"	30th	Signalling exercise carried out with Battery H.Q and Brigade H.Q.	
	"	3Ist	Ordinary Brigade Routine.	

H. Pooley.

Lieut: Colonel, R.F.A.

Commanding 88th Brigade, R.F.A.

2449 Wt. W14957/M90 750,000 1/16 J.B.C. & A. Forms/C.2118/12.

Instructions regarding War Diaries and Intelligence Summaries are contained in F. S. Regs., Part II. and the Staff Manual respectively. Title Pages will be prepared in manuscript.

WAR DIARY
or
~~INTELLIGENCE SUMMARY~~

(Erase heading not required.)

Army Form C. 2118.

88 Bde R.F.A. Vol 21

Place	Date	Hour	Summary of Events and Information	Remarks and references to Appendices
POLINCOVE (2nd Army Training Area)	April	1st.	Brigade Training programme, cleaning up, re-fitting, re-equiping etc carried out. (5a)	HAZEBROUCK 1/100,000.
	"	2nd	" " " " " "	"
	"	3rd	" " " " " "	"
	"	4th	" ", and preparations made to move up to the forward area tomorrow, 5th.	"
	"	5th	Brigade marched from POLINCOVE, via NORDAUSQUE - MOULLE - ST.MARTIN - S. of ST.OMER - ARQUES to CAMPAGNE LES WARLECQUES and there billetted for the night.	"
	"	6th	March resumed via EBBLINGHEM - HAZEBROUCK - ST.SYLVESTRE - CAESTRE to Squares W.9, W.10., W.15 and W.16	Sheet 27 1/40,000
	"	7th	March resumed via CAESTRE - BAILLEUL - LOCRE to squares M.5 and M.11 and Batteries took over the Wagon Lines which had been vacated by 180th F.A. Bde: as follows:- "A"/88 wagon line at M 5 C 2 3., "B"/88 at M 11 A 2 8., "C"/88 at M 11 C 2 6., "D"/88 at M 11 C 5.5.. Brigade Hd-Qrs established in WESTOUTRE.	Sheet 28 S.W. 1/20,000.
	"	8th	Each battery sent two sections into action during the evening, in positions as follows:- "A"/88 relieved "C"/77 at N 16 A 40 85., "B"/88 relievd "A"/77 at N 10 C 8 0., "C"/88 relieved "B"/77 ~~at~~ with two guns at N 4 D 20 23 and with 4 guns at N 4 B 4 2., "D"/88 relieved "D"/77 with two 4.5" Hows: at N 16B 45 25 and 4 hows: at N 4 C 90 80	" & Sheet WYTSCHAETE 1/10,000.
	"	9th	The remaining Section of each battery moved up into action, and reliefs completed. Brigade H.Q. moved up and established at LA CLYTTE and took over from H.Q. 77th (Army) F.A. Brigade. With batteries 88th Bde: R.F.A. in positions above, and "A"/77 which moved in action at N 10 A 3 8, "C"/77 which moved to N 16 A 49 57, and "D"/77 which moved to N 4 C 0 7, this now formed the DIEPENDAAL ARTILLERY GROUP. Zone of responsibility N 18 B 20.55 - O 7 B 85.62.	Sheet 28 S.W 1/20000 " WYTSCHAETE 1/10,000. "
	"	10th	Registrations of zero and "S.O.S." Lines carried out but was unsatisfactory owing to a high and gusty wind. Between 2.0 pm and 5.0 pm the enemy wire was engaged in N 18 B and a gap 20 yards to 25 yards wide was made at N 18 B 50.45. The enemy bombarded N 4 A & C between 6.0 pm and 8.0 pm after which his artillery was fairly quiet throughout the day. At 11.58 pm the Infantry called for "S.O.S." Barrage as the enemy was heavily shelling front line and supports in N.12.D. The "S.O.S." Barrage was put on from 11.58 pm to 12.16 a.m. Whilst the enemy bombardment lasted, he raided our lines and caused some casualties and two men were found missing, believed taken prisoners.	
	~~xxxxth~~			
	"	11th	Enemy wire at O 7 A 9½ 9½ was attacked and practically no wire was left standing over a front of about 30 yards N.E. from this point. Enemy wire at N 18 B 5 5 was also attacked with fair results. At Infantry's request we retaliated on ONRAET FARM amd O 13 D 64 50, as he had been heavily shelling N 11 A Central.	
	"	12th	Some registrations were carried out on N 18 B 2 6., O 7 C 35.50., O 17.A.98.05 etc. and enemy wire was attacked at O 7 B 4 3½., N 18 B 55 60 and N 18 B 55 70. which appeared successful.	

2449 Wt. W14957/M90 750,000 1/16 J.B.C. & A. Forms/C.2118/12.

Instructions regarding War Diaries and Intelligence Summaries are contained in F. S. Regs., Part II. and the Staff Manual respectively. Title Pages will be prepared in manuscript.

WAR DIARY

or

~~INTELLIGENCE SUMMARY~~

(Erase heading not required.)

Army Form C. 2118.

Place	Date	Hour	Summary of Events and Information	Remarks and references to Appendices
	April	12th	(contd;) A gap of 20 yards to 25 yards wide was made in enemy wire at O 7 B $2\frac{1}{4}$ $2\frac{1}{2}$ and the wire about point N 18 B 55.60 seemed to be pretty nearly destroyed.	Sheet WYTSCHAETE 28 S.W 2 1/10,000
	"	13th	Further registrations and calibrations were carried out and wire again attacked at O 7 B 3 3 and a gap 30 yards and 15 yards either side of this point, was cut. The enemy was active against RIDGE WOOD and VIERSTRAAT during the morning and VIERSTRAAT was again shelled in the afternoon.	
	"	14th	Only normal artillery fire was carried out by both sides during the day. On orders that 177th Brigade R.F.A. would join DIEPENDAAL ARTILLERY GROUP as reinforcing Batteries, "C"/177 Battery came into action during the evening at N 4 C 8 4.	
	"	15th	Firing on selected objectives was carried out during the day and enemy artillery was below normal. The remainder of the 177th Bde: R.F.A. came into action during the evening in possitions as follows:- "A"/177 at N 4 C 5 0., "B"/177 at N 4 C 5 3., "D"/177 at N 4 B 9 8.	
	"	16th	During the day registrations were carried out in a desultory mannar in connection with a forthcoming Infantry raid. Enemy lightly shelled VIERSTRAAT and RIDGE WOOD for which we retaliated on O 13 B 6.8 - 2.3 "A"/77 "C"/77 "D"/77 and all Batteries 177th Bde: withdrew to the Wagon Lines.	
	"	17th	Further registrations were carried out during the day, and a timbered construction at O 8 D 7 0 with trench leading to it was demolished during the afternoon. EVANS FARM and LOUWAEGE FARM were also engaged by us. Enemy artillery was exceedingly quiet throughout the day.	
	"	18th	During the day OBSTRUCTION TRENCH in O 7 D, Railway in OOSTTAVERNE WOOD, O 7 C 5 1 and O 7 C 4 5 were amongst the objectives engaged by the Group and O 13 A 20 98 was engaged by 4.5" Hows: in the evening and several direct hits obtained. An active hostile Trenhh Mortar in BOIS QUARANTE was engaged and caused to desist. Enemy artillery again very quiet.	
	"	19th	Movement at O 13 A 4 4, dug-outs at O 7 D $5\frac{1}{2}$ 3 and Trench Junction O 13 B 64.60 were engaged during the day. Hostile artillery lightly shelled Areas N 7 D., N 17 D and N 23 C.	
	"	20th	The usual firing on selected objectives took place during the day, some of these being:- M.G. emplacement O 7 C 7 9 and N 18 B 52 40, barricade at N.18.B.50.35 and house at O 8 D 9 4. Hostile artillery showed increased artillery fire shelling RIDGE WOOD, DICKEBUSCH and P & O Trench with 105 mm Howitzers. N 9 D and N 10.C were shelled with 150 mm Hows: in the afternoon.	
	"		Between 7.15 pm and 8.35 pm the enemy very heavily shelled our front line system with guns of all calibres and at 7.30 p.m. on the Infantry sending out "S.O.S." Signals the Group opened fire on its S.O.S. Lines and stopped at 8.30 p.m.	
	"	21st	Hostile M.G.s and rifle fire was very active against our aeroplanes and to stop this the Group fire on trenches O 13 A 80 60 - O 7 D 35 15, suspected M.G. at O 13 A 4 3 which was successful. Registration with balloon was carried out in the afternoon. Enemy artillery was very active against Battery position in N 9 C and house N 11 C 50 45.	

Instructions regarding War Diaries and Intelligence Summaries are contained in F. S. Regs., Part II. and the Staff Manual respectively. Title Pages will be prepared in manuscript.

WAR DIARY
or
~~INTELLIGENCE SUMMARY~~

(Erase heading not required.)

Army Form C. 2118.

Place	Date	Hour	Summary of Events and Information	Remarks and references to Appendices
LA CLYTTE.	April	~~21st~~ 22nd	During the day registration with balloons was carried out and other targets engaged were:- Movement at O 9 C 50 75 and O 9 C 45 90., Hostile battery at O 21 A 1 2, O 3 D 85.25., Barricade across SUNKEN ROAD at N 18 B 55 23. etc. Enemy artillery was very inactive, shelling VIERSTRAAT with only a few rounds 105 mm How: Enemy aeroplanes were fairly active, one attacking one of our Kite Balloons and forcing it to descend.	Sheet 28 S.W. 1/20,000 and WYTSCHAETE 1/10,000.
	"	23rd	During the day, registration with aeroplane was carried out on Cross Roads O 20 C 18 80 and O 20 D 40 43 which was satisfactory. A reported enemy M.G. at N.18.B.5.6 was engaged and also hostile battery at O 27 A 10 00. Eight wireless "N.F." Calls were received and responded to. Hostile artillery showed considerable activity, cheifly against VIERSTRAAT, DICKEBUSCH, YORK ROAD and Cross Roads O 20 D 40 43. During the night "A"/87, "B"/87 and "D"/87 moved into action and joined the DIEPENDAAL ARTILLERY GROUP, taking up positions as follows:- "A"/87 (4 guns) at N 10 A 3 8., "B"/87 2 guns at N 4 C 5 2 and 2 guns at N 4 C 8 3, "D"/87 (6 hows) at N 4 C 0 8.	
	"	24th	Registrations were carried out during the day and RENTRY FARM, LOUWAEGE FARM, Railway Track ~~[illegible]~~ through GRAND BOIS, O 13 A 5 3., O 13 B 1 8 and O 7 D 4 1 were engaged. Hostile artillery fire was normal.	
	"	25th	Registration on MARTENS FARM, N.BRICKSTACK O 13 C 27 81 and Trench Junction O 7 D 3 5 were carried out and Suspected T.M. at O 13 A 3 7., movement at O 2 D 8 3 were also engaged. Enemy shelled DICKEBUSCH, N 11 C & D., N 12 D during the day and the trenches of Left Coy. Left Battalion with Heavy Minenwerfers. During the evening "C"/87 Battery also came into action and joined the DIEPENDAAL GROUP, coming into action at N 10 C 7 2 (with 4 guns)	
	"	26th	"B" Battery 88th Bde: R.F.A. moved from its position at N 10 C 8 0 to position at N 9 D 0 0 being relieved in the former position by "B"/180th F.A. Bde: during the evening. For this purpose "C"/87 Battery took over the defence of the line from "B"/88 Battery. During the day we engaged Working party at N 12 D 44 10, movement at O 8 B 8 o & O 8 B 5 9 & O 7 C 30 25, Suspected O.Ps in O 14 and trenches & C.Ts in front of GRAND BOIS. We also retaliated on OBIT SUPPORT TRENCH and Hostile Battery at O 17 C 75 25. Night firing programme on Roads, Cross Roads and selected objectives was carried out. Hostile artillery has been quiet throught the day.	
	"	27th	"B" Battery 88th Bde: registered from its new position at N 9 D 0 0 and on completion of all arrangements took over the defence of the line again from "C"/87 Battery, which then became a re-inforcing battery. During the day we engaged hostile battery at O 5 C 75 25, Screen at O 14 C 35 05 Dump at O 20 A 3 1. Suspected O.P. O 19 B 6.6 etc. Hostile artillery has been again very quiet.	

Army Form C. 2118.

Instructions regarding War Diaries and Intelligence Summaries are contained in F. S. Regs., Part II. and the Staff Manual respectively. Title Pages will be prepared in manuscript.

WAR DIARY
or
INTELLIGENCE SUMMARY
(Erase heading not required.)

Place	Date	Hour	Summary of Events and Information	Remarks and references to Appendices
LA CLYTTE	April	28th	During the day O 19 B 9.9., Hostile battery O 5 C 75 25, Railway O 13 A O 5 - O 13 A 5 1, suspected M.G. at O 13 B 20 95., movement at O 7 C 35 50. A Wireless Zone Call received in the evening was responded to. Night firing on Cross roads, and selected objectives was carried out.	Sheet 28 S.W. 1/20,000 and WYTSCHAETE 10,000
	"	29th	On orders being received that 19th Divisional Arty. would be relieved by 16th Divisional Arty: "A"/87, "B"/87 and "D"/87 Batteries withdrew from action during the day and marchedback to their Wagon Line. "C"/87 Battery withdrew from action during the evening. During the day LOUWAEGE FARM, OBTUSE CRESCENT Cross Roads O 20 A 8 3. Road junctions O 15 A 3½ 1½ & O 8 D 45 50 and suspected O.P.at O 8 C 7.½ were engaged and night firing programme was carried out. The enemy heavily shelled RIDGE WOOD and the vicinity of RENINGHELST.	
	"	30th	During the day the Group engaged battery positions at O 10 B 1 2 and O 20 D 9 5½, Cross Roads O 20 D 4 4., and O 20 A 3.8. and O 9 D 3 3. Little hostile shelling was observed. In the evening 1 Section of each battery was relieved in action by I section of the corresponding Battery 180th F.A. Bde:	

[signature]

Lieutenant Colonel, R.F.A.

Commanding 88th Brigade R.F.A.

2449 Wt. W14957/M90 750,000 1/16 J.B.C. & A. Forms/C.2118/12.

Instructions regarding War Diaries and Intelligence Summaries are contained in F. S. Regs., Part II. and the Staff Manual respectively. Title Pages will be prepared in manuscript.

WAR DIARY
or
INTELLIGENCE SUMMARY
(Erase heading not required.)

88 Bde RFA Vol 22

Army Form C. 2118.

Place	Date	Hour	Summary of Events and Information	Remarks and references to Appendices
LA CLYTTE.	May	1st	The relief of the remaining 2 sections of each battery by corresponding batteries 180th Bde: R.F.A 16th Divn; was carried out and completed. H.Q. handed over to H.Q. 180th Bde. H.Q and Batteries returned to Wagon Lines. The 1 section of each battery relieved yesterday moved up into action, as follows:- "A"/88 relieved "A"/103 (23rd Divn) at I 15 A 75 40, "B"/88 relieved "B"/103 at I 15 B 90 85., "C"/88 relieved "C"/103 at I 15 B 35 45., "D"/88 relieved "D"/103 at CONVENT, YPRES I 14 A 75 45.	Sheets 28 SW 1/20,000 ----- WYTSCHAETE 1/10,000 -----
LILLE GATE YPRES.	"	2nd	Reliefs of remaining sections of 103rd Bde: at above positions and of H.Q./103 at LILLE GATE, YPRES completed during the evening. Enemy very heavily shelled vicinity of LILLE GATE from 6.0 - 9.0 pm with about 500 rounds. All wagon lines are now at	28 N.W 1/20,000 -----
	"	3rd	Registrations of Zero, "S.O.S." and Night Lines carried out during day. Enemy again heavily shelled vicinity of LILLE GATE with about 200 rounds including gas shells. YPRES was intermittently shelled throughout day and night.	ZILLEBEKE 1/10,000 ------
RAILWAY DUG-OUTS at I 21 C 0 8	"	4th	Further registrations carried out. H.Q. moved from LILLE GATE and established in RAILWAY DUG-OUTS at I 21 C 0 8. Enemy artillery was normal but YPRES and back areas were intermittently shelled during day.	
	"	5th	Some registrations and calibrations were carried out. Enemy artillery was normal except for shelling of YPRES during day and slight shelling of SHRAPNEL CORNER.	
	"	6th	" " " " "	
	"	7th	At 9.30 am enemy opened very heavy enfilade fire on RAILWAY DUG-OUTS I 21 C 0 8 and vicinity about 1500 rounds 4.2" and 5.9" being fired. This ceased at 1.40 p.m. Considerable damage was done, communications were cut and several dug-out shelters destroyed. Several casualties were caused to Infantry about DUG-OUTS. All communications O.K. at 2.0 pm. During the evening orders received that all guns of 2nd Army (except 12") would fire at intense rate for 5 mins. to stop enemy shelling of back areas, from 8.45 - 8.50 p.m. The Brigade engaged tramway from DUMP J 25 C 9 2 to MOUNT SORREL at intense rate. Enemy retaliated heavily on Centre & Left Battalion front systems but there was no shelling of back areas. This programme was repeated from 11.0 - 11.5 pm and all was quiet throughout the night.	
	"	8th	During the day we retaliated, at Infantry's request, on German 2nd line trenches in I 30 C, We engaged enemy wire at I 30 C 3 7 - 3 7½ with good effect. Hostile arty: was very active against LILLE GATE, MENIN GATE, YPRES, trenches & tracks in vicinity of ZILLEBEKE, also TUILLERIES and I 20 Central.	

2449 Wt. W14957/M90 750,000 1/16 J.B.C. & A. Forms/C.2118/12.

Army Form C. 2118.

Instructions regarding War Diaries and Intelligence Summaries are contained in F. S. Regs., Part II. and the Staff Manual respectively. Title Pages will be prepared in manuscript.

WAR DIARY
or
INTELLIGENCE SUMMARY
(Erase heading not required.)

Place	Date	Hour	Summary of Events and Information	Remarks and references to Appendices
RAILWAY DUG-OUTS.	May	9th	We retaliated on J 25 A 6 6., N 25 D 2 8., J 25 C 7½ 3½., Enemy heavily shelled YPRES, MENIN GATE & Vicinity, and I 15 B 8 8. Hostile Trench Mortars were active against out front line in J 24 B at 10 am and 4.30 pm cutting wire at these points. Hostile balloons were up all day. At 9.25 pm enemy opened a bombardment on our front line, and on "S.O.S." Rocket Signals being sent up by our infantry, we opened our S.O.S. Barrage until 9.54 p.m. when all was quiet until 3.45 a.m. when he again commenced and we put on our S.O.S. barrage till 4.40 a.m. During 1 of these periods our front post No: 14 was entered and the occupants probably taken prisoners. The enemy was neither seen to enter or leave the post.	Sheets:- 28 N W --- ZILLEBEKE 1/10,000
	"	10th	During afternoon we retaliated on I 30 D 9½ 5, J 25 C 7½ 3½ and 2nd line trenches in I 30 A & B. Hostile shelling was heavy on BLAU POORT FARM, YPRES, I 14 D., and battery positions I 15 A 75 40 causing casualties at the position. During the evening one section of each battery was relieved by a section of corresponding batteries 103rd Bde: R.F.A. 23rd Division.	
	"	11th	We retaliated on 2nd line in I 30 A & B at infantry's request. From 7 - 8 am enemy heavily shelled LILLE GATE and from 7.30 - 10.0 am SHRAPNEL CORNER & Vicinity with about 300 rounds 4." & 5.9". Throughout the morning until 2.10 p.m. enemy bombarded RAILWAY DUG-OUTS with about 1000 rounds. He also shelled RUDKIN HOUSE, DAVIDSON STREET, ZILLEBEKE STREET. During the morning Battery Wagon Lines moved to M 2 D 8 0. During the evening relief of H.Q. and Batteries by 103rd Bde: was completed. Batteries returned to their new Wagon Line and Headquarters to G 24 B 8 8.	
Nr WESTCOUTRE	"	12th	Bde: H.Q. moved and established near WESTCOUTRE and the Brigade is now in reserve.	Sheet 28 SW 1/20,000
	"	14th)		
	"	15th)		
	"	16th)	Ordinary Brigade Routine carried out, including Battery Gun Drills.	
	"	17th)		
	"	18th)		
	"	19th)		
	"	20th	Ordinary Routine. In accordance with 19th D.A. Orders "D"/88 Battery moved its H.Q. and 1 Section into action at N 4 B 9½ 9½ and came under orders of DIEPENDAAL GROUP H.Q. for tactical purposes.	
	"	21st	Ordinary Brigade Routine.	
	"	22nd	" " " . During the night another section of "D"/88 moved into action at N 4 B 9½ 9½.	
	"	23rd	During the evening, in accordance with 19th D.A. orders, "B"/88 Battery H.Q. & 1 Section moved up into action at N 4 B 17 05 and came under the orders of DIEPENDAAL GROUP H.Q. for tactical purposes.	
	"	24th	During the evening the remaining section of "D"/88 Battery moved into action at N 4 B 9½ 9½.	

2449 Wt. W14957/M90 750,000 1/16 J.B.C. & A. Forms/C.2118/12.

Instructions regarding War Diaries and Intelligence Summaries are contained in F. S. Regs., Part II. and the Staff Manual respectively. Title Pages will be prepared in manuscript.

WAR DIARY
or
INTELLIGENCE SUMMARY
(Erase heading not required.)

Army Form C. 2118.

Place	Date	Hour	Summary of Events and Information	Remarks and references to Appendices
Near WESTOUTRE	May	24th	(continued) The remaining two sections of "B"/88 Battery also moved into action at N 4 B 17 05. and "B"/88 is now being used for wire-cutting purposes.	Sheet 28 S W 1/20,000
	"	25th	Ordinary Brigade Routine for H.Q. "A"/88 & "C"/88½ H.Q moved to W.L at M 2 D 8 0.	
LA CLYTTE. N 7 C 3 5.	"	26th	Headquarters with Wagon Line moved up and established at LA CLYTTE, N 7 C 3 5 and became H.Q. LEFT GROUP, DIEPENDAAL SECTOR consisting of "B"/88 and "D"/88 Batteries, "C"/87 and "C"/77. Night firing tasks carried out.	WYTSCHAETE 1/10,000
	"	27th	Wire-cutting was carried out on OBIT SUPPORT, OBLIGE SWITCH, OBSTRUCTION TRENCH, 0 13 B 9 1 to 0 13 A 5 8 with good results, and gap in enemy wire between 0 7 B 85 62 - 0 7 B 80 56 [illegible] and 0 13 A 95 99 - 0 13 A 95 90 were cleared and enlarged. Movement at LOUWAEGE FARM was engaged. Enemy heavily shelling HALLEBAST DUMP and vicinity during early morning but was quiet throughout day. Night firing on "tasks" and keeping open gaps in enemy wire carried out. During the evening "C"/88 Battery moved up into action at its Magnum Opus position N 5 A 1 0. Enemy active between 9.0 pm and 3.15 a.m. on RIDGE WOOD, VIERSTRAAT, and N 4 B & D.	
	"	28th	Wire-cutting carried out on OBLIGE SWITCH and 0 7 B 6 5 - 0 7 B 7 6 - 0 7 B 7 3 and some registrations. Enemy artillery quiet throught day. "D"/88 moved from N 4 B 9½ 9½ to its Magnum Opus position N 5 A 22 60. Night firing carried out on "tasks" and gaps in enemy wire.	
	"	29th	Wire-cutting carried out at 0 7 B 3 3 on OBSTRUCTION SWITCH and registrations on ZERO HOUSE and S.O.S Lines. Gaps in wire about ONRAET WOOD were engaged. Enemy artillery was chiefly directed against RIDGE WOOD, VIERSTRAAT, DICKEBUSH, HALLEBAST CORNER and vicinity. Night firing programme carried out. "B"/88 Battery moved from its present position to its Magnum Opus position N 5 C 03 77 and "A"/88 Battery moved from its Wagon Line into action to its Magnum Opus position N 5 C 42 27. The LEFT ARTY: GROUP now consists of Batteries 88th, 150th, and 232nd F.A. Brigades, & is divided into 2 sub-groups. H.Q. & Batteries 232nd F.A. Bde:, "A"/88 and "B"/88 forming "C" Sub-group; H.Q. & Batteries 150th F.A. Bde:, "C"/88 and "D"/88 forming "D" Sub-group.	
	"	30th	During the morning a "Practice Barrage" as per X Corps Orders was carried out. Registrations were carried out. Enemy artillery was only moderately active throughtout day. Night firing carried out.	
	"	31st	Wire-cutting carried out from 0 7 B 3 4 - 0 7 B 5 5, OPTIC TRENCH 0 7 D 4 5 - 4.9., 0 7 C 5 7, & OBIT TRENCH & SUPPORT. Enemy artillery quiet during day firing 100 rounds 4.2" into VIERSTRAAT. Night firing programme carried out.	

H Covey

Lieut: Colonel, R.F.A.
Commanding 88th Brigade, R. F. A.

2449 Wt. W14957/M90 750,000 1/16 J.B.C. & A. Forms/C.2118/12.

Instructions regarding War Diaries and Intelligence Summaries are contained in F. S. Regs., Part II. and the Staff Manual respectively. Title Pages will be prepared in manuscript.

WAR DIARY
or
INTELLIGENCE SUMMARY
(Erase heading not required.)

Army Form C. 2118.

88 Bde R F A 19
Vol 23

Place	Date	Hour	Summary of Events and Information	Remarks and references to Appendices
LA CLYTTE	JUNE	1st	During the day batteries engaged targets as per Bombardment Programme in connection with forthcoming offensive, including all enemy wire, trenches, strong points, dug-outs, etc. These ~~xxxxx~~ included OBJECT SWITCH, OBIT TRENCH & SUPPORT, OBSTRUCTION TRENCH [illegible] SWITCH, OBTUSE CRESCENT, ONRAET WOOD, OBSTINATE TRENCH, EVANS FARM, OBEY SUPPORT, GRAND BOIS, PETIT BOIS, MARTENS FARM. At 6.0 pm a practice barrage was carried out. Night firing carried out, keeping gaps in wire open and engaging tracks and approaches.	WYTSCHAETE 1/10,000 -and- Sheet 28 SW 1/20,000
	"	2nd	Bombardment as above continued, and similar night firing.	
	"	3rd	" " " " " " " . AT 11.45 am and 3.0 pm practice barrages were carried out. Night firing as above.	
FARM at N 3 B 4 2½	"	4th	Bombardment continued. H.Q. moved to Battle H.Q. at Farm N 3 B 40 25. Night firing as above.	
	"	5th	Bombardment continued. From 3.0 pm to 3.25 pm barrage was put on in connection with raid by 56th and 58th Infantry Brigades during which about 80 prisoners were taken. Night firing carried out.	
	"	6th	Bombardment continued during day. M.G. emplacement at O 8 C 85 80 was destroyed. All arrangements completed for advancing on "Z" day at Zero hour plus 20 mins: to forward positions. "Z" Day notified as tomorrow 7th inst. and Zero hour 3.10 A.M. Night firing carried on without pause until that hour.	
	"	7th	At 3.10 a.m. the Barrage for the Offensive was opened and carried on in accordance with Barrage Tables. The Infantry operations were successful, all objectives being taken. At 7.0 a.m. all teams were at position of assembly (N 2 D 6 3) ready to move forward. At 8.30 a.m. the Brigade advanced to positions already reconnoitred, viz. H.Q. N 6 D 3½ 6½., "A"/88 O 1 C 3½ 6½., "B"/88, O 1 C 4½ 7½., "C"/88 O 1 C 5½ 8½., "D"/88 O 1 C 3 9. At 11.0 a.m. move was completed and Batteries were ready to fire. A few registrations were carried out preparatory to a further advance by the Infantry. At 3.10 PM barrage in support of Infantry programme was opened, when final objectives (including COSTTAVERNE) were gained. During afternoon Wagon Lines were moved up to N 2 D 6 3. Throughout the night firing was carried out on tracks and places likely to hold enemy.	
	"	8th	At 5.55 pm Zone Calls ~~xxx~~ were received that enemy were massing at O 24 C 9 9, and responded to. Day passed quietly. At 8.40 PM batteries opened on S.O.S. Lines as enemy artillery was very active and large numbers of enemy were reported opposite our front. This fire was very effective. Throughout the night firing on roads and tracks and placed likely to hold enemy was again carried out.	
	"	9th	At 7.0 am Zone Calls were received and responded to. During the day registrations were confirmed and continued. All movement seen was engaged. Hostile aeroplanes were very active during the morning, but were engaged by our aeroplanes. Hostile artillery was quiet. Usual night firing took place.	

Army Form C. 2118.

WAR DIARY
or
INTELLIGENCE SUMMARY

(Erase heading not required.)

Instructions regarding War Diaries and Intelligence Summaries are contained in F. S. Regs., Part II. and the Staff Manual respectively. Title Pages will be prepared in manuscript.

Place	Date	Hour	Summary of Events and Information	Remarks and references to Appendices
BEGGARS'S REST HEDGE N 6 D 3½ 6½	June	10th	Some registrations carried out and movement and selected objectives engaged. Hostile artillery active on front systems. At 11.30 pm batteries put on S.O.S. Barrage at Infantry's request as as enemy artillery was heavily shelling front system. Night firing on CANAL BRIDGE, approaches etc.	WYTSCHAETE 1/10,000 -and- Sheet 28 SW 1/20,000
	"	11th	Registrations carried out. At 3.10 pm we retaliated on GREEN WOOD O 17 A. Enemy shelled area O 15, O 16 A & C with all calibres. Considerable enemy aerial activity during day. Night firing as above carried out.	
	"	12th	Day passed very quietly. Night firing carried out.	
	"	13th	In addition to registrations, Buildings O 17 C 6 6, 8.8., O 17 D O 8, & GROENLIND CABARET were engaged and much damaged. On three occasions during afternoon we retaliated for heavy enemy shelling. In the evening enemy shelled ST. ELOI, O 8 A 5 5, OOSTTAVERNE WOOD and DENYS WOOD. Night firing programme carried out.	
	"	14th	Registration and calibration carried out during morning. GREEN WOOD, O 17 C 40 99., & GROENLIND CABARET again engaged with good results. Enemy shelled OOSTTAVERNE WOOD, RAVINE WOOD & O 15 A. From 7.30 - 8.30 pm batteries barraged as per 19th D.A. orders in support of Infantry Raid. Enemy immediately opened barrage on front line and searched forward area. Considerable enemy aerial activity during evening. Night firing carried out.	
	"	15th	Targets in O 17 C were engaged and registrations on KORTEWILDE. On four occasions during afternoon and evening we retaliated for enemy shelling beyond our front line. Enemy also shelled WYTSCHAETE, CHRAET WOOD, OOSTTAVERNE WOOD, RAVINE WOOD and O 8 A during day. During night we engaged houses in O 17 B & D. Intermittent enemy shelling during evening and night of forward area and vicinity of O 15 B 1 4. During night "D"/88 Battery moved to new position at O 4 A 6 0	
	"	16th	Quiet day. From 9.45 - 10.40 pm in response to S.O.S. Call we put on S.O.S. barrage and searched forward area, as enemy was shelling our front line and Ridge behind O 15 A & B. Many fires were observed in enemy lines during evening. Night firing programme carried out.	
	"	17th	During day batteries registered on houses, buildings etc for identification purposes. Enemy less active during the day. Night firing carried out.	
	"	18th	Registration on GREEN WOOD and Road running N.W. in P 13 & joining Main road at P 13 B 4 7, was carried out. Enemy artillery normal. Night firing on usual objectives carried out.	
	"	19th	"B"/88, "C"/88 & "D"/88 were relieved by corresponding batteries 180th F.A. Bde: (personnel only) between 2.0 pm and 6.0 pm. Personnel of "B"/88, "C"/88, "D"/88 proceeded and took over guns in action of 180th Bde:, the guns of both Brigades being in action during period of relief. H.Q./88 was relieved by H.Q./180 at 8.0 pm. Between 9.0 pm and 4.0 am H.Q./88, "B"/88, "C"/88 "D"/88 withdrew to wagon lines. "A"/88 Battery remained in action under orders of 180th F.A. Bde:	
M 8 C O 4.	"	20th	Brigade (less A/88) marched via CHEAPSIDE, LA-CLYTTE - WESTOUTRE to reserve area. Wagon lines about WESTOUTRE. H.Q. established at M 8 C O 4.	

2449 Wt. W14957/M90 750,000 1/16 J.B.C. & A. Forms/C.2118/12.

Army Form C. 2118.

Instructions regarding War Diaries and Intelligence Summaries are contained in F. S. Regs., Part II. and the Staff Manual respectively. Title Pages will be prepared in manuscript.

WAR DIARY
or
INTELLIGENCE SUMMARY

(Erase heading not required.)

Place	Date	Hour	Summary of Events and Information	Remarks and references to Appendices
M 8 C 0 4	JUNE to JUNE	21st to 24th	Ordinary Brigade Routine. General cleaning up, re-fitting and re-equipping carried out.	WYTSCHAETE 1/10,000 -and- Sheet 28 SW 1/20,000
	JUNE	25th	Inspection of Brigade by G.O.C. 19th Division.	
	"	26th	Ordinary Brigade Routine.	
	"	27th	Relief of 180th Bde: R.F.A. (personnel only, guns being left in position) commenced as follows:- "B"/88 relieved "B"/180 2 guns at O 7 B 30 60, & 1 at N 12 D 35 30., "D"/88 relieved "D"/180 2 guns at O 7 A 6 0 & 1 at N 12 D 05'55. Completed by 12 noon.	
N 18 A 2 5.	"	28th	Relief of "B"/180 and "D"/180 at O 7 B 30 60 and O 7 A 6 0, respectively, completed. H.Q. took over from H.Q./180 at N 18 A 20 50. "A"/88 still in action came under orders of this Brigade, and ~~xkxx~~ "B"/315 Bde: having relieved "C"/180 with 5 guns at O 7 B 6 7 and 1 at O 7 C 00 40 also came under this Brigade for tactical purposes. "C"/88 Battery remained at its wagon line near WESTOUTRE pending orders to proceed to 2nd Army Arty: School. Wagon lines were taken over from 180th Bde: as follows:- H.Q. at M 22 D 1 8, "B"/88 M 21 C 6 8, "D"/88 M 26 D 3 8. Night firing on Roads, Houses, Tracks etc carried out.	
	"	29th	Registration and calibrations carried out. Hostile artillery exceptionally active in O 7 D and vicinity with 10.5 cm shells. Enemy aircraft active throughout the day. Night firing carried out.	
	"	30th	During the day selected objectives were engaged. Enemy artillery and aircraft much less active. Night firing programme carried out.	

[illegible signature] Major R.F.A.
Commandi[illegible] [illegible]th Brigade R.F.A.

2449 Wt. W14957/M90 750,000 1/16 J.B.C. & A. Forms/C.2118/12.

Instructions regarding War Diaries and Intelligence Summaries are contained in F. S. Regs., Part II, and the Staff Manual respectively. Title pages will be prepared in manuscript.

WAR DIARY
or
INTELLIGENCE SUMMARY.
(Erase heading not required.)

88 Fa Bde
vol 24

Army Form C. 2118.

Place	Date	Hour	Summary of Events and Information	Remarks and references to Appendices
	1917.			
N 18 A 20 50	July 1st		Owing to re-adjustment of Corps Zones, moves by batteries, as follows, took plase. During night 30th June/1st July B/88 moved to O 8 A 6 2. During night 1st/2nd "D"/88 moved to new position O 8 D 2 7. During day registrations carried out and engaged selected objectives. Hostile artillery below normal Night firing carried out on roads and tracks and HOUTHEM.	WYTSCHAETE 1/10,000 Sheet 28 SW 1/20,000
	" 2nd		Normal day. Considerable aerial activity on both sides and many enemy balloons were up. During night "B"/315 (under orders of this Bde:) moved to position O 8 C 2 6. A/88 remains in position O 7 D 2 7. Night firing as above carried out.	
	" 3rd		B/88 and D/88 wagon lines moved to N 20 C 2 8 and N 20 A 5 9 respectively. Registrations carried out during the day. Enemy artillery fairly quiet, engaging GRAND BOIS between 7.o - 8.30 a.m. Night firing on tracks in O 18 A & B, O 11 D, O 12 D and Canal Bridges.	
	" 4th		Registrations and calibration carried out. We engaged Trenches P 13 B 3 6 and reported Battalion H.Q. P 13 b 7 7 causing considerable damage. Buildings and dug-outs in Group zone also engaged.	WERVICQ 1/10,000
	"		Usual night firing programme carried out.	
	" 5th		During day movement at O 18 A 45 40 (gun-pit) was engaged and houses, huts, dug-outs etc in O 18 B & D. Enemy artillery much more active. Considerable movement observed behind enemy's lines. Night firing on HOUTHEM CROSS RDS, Canal crossing P 13 A 7 6, COPSE FARM, huts roads, etc.	
	" 6th		We engaged selected targets during day and responded to "N.F." Call at P 14 D 9 1 obtaining several direct hits. H.Q./88 wagon line moved to N 19 B 2 3. Considerable aerial activity during morning and evening. Enemy artillery normal. At 8 pm 4.5" Hows: engaged enemy gun at P 14 D 8 1. From 9.30 - 11.30 pm enemy heavily shelled ROSE WOOD, RAVINE WOOD and also on our right and fired many rockets, but no action resulted. Enemy 'plane flewxlow over his lines at this time.	
	" 7th		Registrations carried out, and enemy movement was engaged. Hostile artillery was active against BOIS QUARANTE, O 7 A and N 17 B. "A"/88 moved 5 guns to position O 7 B 9 0 and left 1 lone gun in present position. Enemy aircraft were very active during the evening. Night firing programme carried out.	
	" 8th		Usual firing on selected objectives took place during day, and night firing on buildings, huts tracks, etc.	
	" 9th		During afternoon D/88 bombarded buildings O 17 C 6 6, O 17 C 9 8, O 17 B 9 3 and dug-out O 17 C 15 30 in connection with the advance of our line to-night, by the Infantry. Selected objectives in Group zone were also engaged during the day, and the usual night firing took place.	
	" 10th		Selected objectives, enemy movement at P 19 B 5 9, dug-outs in O 12 C were engaged during day. The flashes of many hostile batteries were spotted during the day. Night firing programme carried out.	

D. D. & L., London, E.C. (A7883) Wt W809/M1672 350,000 4/17 Sch. 52a Forms/C/2118/14

Instructions regarding War Diaries and Intelligence Summaries are contained in F. S. Regs., Part II, and the Staff Manual respectively. Title pages will be prepared in manuscript.

WAR DIARY
or
INTELLIGENCE SUMMARY.
(Erase heading not required.)

Army Form C. 2118.

Place	Date	Hour	Summary of Events and Information	Remarks and references to Appendices
N 18 A 2 5	July	11th	During afternoon personnel of A/88 were relieved by A/46, and A/88 took over guns from A/46 at wagon lines. During evening 1 Section B/46 moved into action at O 8 C 15 20 and with A/46 came under orders of 88th Bde: for tactical purposes. The usual firing took place during day. There was much aerial activity on both sides.	
	"	12th	A/88 moved to wagon line at M 21C O 8. During the night, remaining sections of B/46 moved into action. We engaged hostile battery at O 20 A 40 65 and other selected objectives. Usual night firing took place.	
	"	13th	Quiet day. We silenced enemy gun at P 20 A 10 85. At 10.30 pm enemy heavily shelled O 15 and O 21.	
GRAND BOIS.	"	14th	Quiet day. Headquarters moved to GRAND BOIS O 13 B O 9. From 10.15 pm - 2330 am enemy shelled CATTEAU FARM and vicinity with several hundred shells, including gas shell.	
	"	15th	Between 10 am and 2 pm D/88 bombarded BOMB FARM O 18 C 7 9 with 200 rounds in connection with Infantry raid tonight. Enemy movement and selected objectives were engaged during day. Hostile artillery normal. At 10.30 pm we retaliated at Infantry's request. Night firing on huts, tracks, roads, buildings, etc. In connection with forthcoming offensive, batteries	
	"		prepared alternative positions already selected, and 1 section B/88 moved to its alternative position at O 9 B 5 O during the night.	
	"	16th	A/88 moved to wagon line at N 14 A 8 O during morning. In conjunction with heavies, 18-prs engaged GREEN FARM O 17 B 35 42 and SPUD FARM O 18 B 20 83 during day. Enemy artillery quiet. Considerable aerial activity. During night A/88 relieved A/46 at O 7 B 9 O and A/46 moved to new position and came under orders of Right Group. Usual night firing took place.	
	"	17th	During day we engaged SPUD FARM, Wire in O 18 B which was much damaged, houses and dug-outs O 17 B 9 3 and the houses were demolished, and enemy movement engaged. Enemy arty: normally active. 18-prs & 4.5" Hows: engaged buildings in connection with Infantry raid on JUNCTION BUILDINGS which was captured. Night firing carried out.	
	"	18th	Selected objectives and movement were engaged , and shoots carried out with heavies. Enemy abnormally quiet until 9.30 pm when he barraged our front line S. of GREEN WOOD and attacked & re-gained JUNCTION BUILDINGS. Our S.O.S. fire was opened immediately he commenced barraging.	
	"	19th	At 3.0 am under cover of our fire, Infantry gained JUNCTION BUILDINGS but enemy again re-gained it at 7.0 am. During day wire in O 18 B was much damaged by our fire and much damage caused by our shoots on buildings etc. Enemy very quiet but fired 200 gas shells on BOIS QUARANTE. Night firing carried out.	
	"	20th	Daily bombardment programme carried out. Between 4.45 - 6.0 pm enemy fired about 200 shells on area O 7 B and O 13 A. Night firing programme carried out.	

D. D. & L., London, E.C. (A7883) Wt W8o9/M1672 350,000 4/17 Sch. 52a Forms/C/2118/14

Army Form C. 2118.

WAR DIARY
or
INTELLIGENCE SUMMARY.
(Erase heading not required.)

Instructions regarding War Diaries and Intelligence Summaries are contained in F. S. Regs., Part II. and the Staff Manual respectively. Title pages will be prepared in manuscript.

Place	Date	Hour	Summary of Events and Information	Remarks and references to Appendices
GRAND BOIS	July	21st	Wire in O 18 B again engaged, also hostile batteries P 20 A 2 8 & 4.8, THE TWINS, and CANAL between P 7 C O 5 - O 13 A 5 7, was engaged in conjunction with heavies. Hostile Arty: active against CATTEAU FARM and CATEN WOOD in the afternoon. Night firing carried out.	
	"	22nd	Road P 7 B 40 35 - P 8 A 2 1 engaged, also GROENELINDE CABT:, PILL FARM, PILGRIMS FARM%, and other targets in bombardment programme. A practice barrage was carried out at 7.5 pm and infantry gained JUNCTION BLDGS, but enemy regained it later. Night firing programme carried out.	
	"	23rd	At 6.45 am we barraged in conjunction with raid by Division on our right to which enemy replied by barraging S.E. edge of GREEN WOOD. Daily bombardment programme carried out. 18-prs fired with Trench Mortars on dug-outs O 17 D 8 8. Enemy arty: normal but aircraft very active flying low. At 10.0 pm we assisted in barrage in conjunction with raid by 47th Div: on our left. Usual night firing programme.	
	"	24th	Daily bombardment programme carried out. Enemy artillery active against Road in O 8 A. Enemy aircraft flew very low over our lines during early morning, firing into CLIVE TRENCH. Night firing carried out.	
	"	25th	" " " " "	
	"	26th	Daily bombardments and night firing programme carried out. Enemy artillery active against O 8 A during afternoon.	
	"	27th	Daily bombardment programme carried out. B/88 fired with 6" T.M. on GREEN FARM and in retaliation enemy shelled O 10 C & D and RAVINE WOOD. Enemy artillery active against DAMM STRASSE. Night firing carried out.	
	"	28th	At 1.50 am batteries barraged on S.O.S. Lines in response to signals as enemy was heavily shelling on Right Group front. Daily bombardments and night firing programmes carried out.	
	"	29th	At 12.30 AM D/88 carried out gas shell bombardment against KORTEWILDE B/88 firing shrapnel at the same time. THE TWINS, SPUD FARM, COPSE FARM, BOMB FARM, POLL FARM and other objectives were engaged during the day. At 5.0 pm D/88 carried out gas shell bombardment against Canal bank P 7 C 55 10 - P 13 A 75 65, B/88 firing shrapnel at the same time. Hostile artillery active. Night firing programme carried out.	
	"	30th	Bombardment programme and night firing carried out until zero hour on 31st. From 7.0 - 8.35 pm D/88 carried out gas shell bombardment against WARNETON Line O 18 B 1 1 - P 13 A 6 6 supported by 18-prs.	
	"	31st	At 3.50 a, (zero hour) batteries opened barrage in support of the Infantry attack and continued same until conclusion of operations which resulted in Infantry capturing their objective.	

[signature]

Lieut: Colonel, R.F.A.
Commanding 88th Brigade, R.F.A.

D. D. & L., London, E.C. (A7883) Wt W809/M1672 350,000 4/17 Sch 52a Forms/C/2118/14

Instructions regarding War Diaries and Intelligence Summaries are contained in F. S. Regs., Part II. and the Staff Manual respectively. Title pages will be prepared in manuscript.

WAR DIARY
or
INTELLIGENCE SUMMARY.
(Erase heading not required.)

Army Form C. 2118.

88 Bde R.F.A.
Vol 25

Place	Date	Hour	Summary of Events and Information	Remarks and references to Appendices
GRAND BOIS	August 1st		Very quiet day. During the night [illegible] C.9.b.[illegible] Usual night firing [illegible]	[illegible]
	2nd		Quiet throughout the day. [illegible]	
	3rd		[illegible]	
	4th		During the day [illegible]	
	5th		[illegible]	
	6th		[illegible]	
	7th		[illegible]	
	8th		Quiet day. [illegible]	
	9th		Hostile aircraft [illegible]	

D. D. & L., London, E.C.
(A8001) Wt. W1771/M2031 750,000 5/17 Sch. 52 Forms/C2118/14

Instructions regarding War Diaries and Intelligence Summaries are contained in F. S. Regs., Part II. and the Staff Manual respectively. Title pages will be prepared in manuscript.

WAR DIARY
or
INTELLIGENCE SUMMARY.

(Erase heading not required.)

Army Form C. 2118.

Place	Date	Hour	Summary of Events and Information	Remarks and references to Appendices
GRAND BOIS.	August			
	9th		Battery less "C"/87th Battery were relieved by I section of the I23rd Brigade R.F.A.	
	I0th		Remaining Sections and Bde: Hd-Qrs relieved and Command of the Group handed over to O.C. I23rd Brigade R.F.A.	
	IIth		The Brigade marched from their wagon lines via LOCRE - BAILLEUL - VIEUX BERQUIN to billets about LA CAUDESCURE K.IC.d.2.2.	Sheet 36 A. I/40,000.
	I2th to 20th		Ordinary Brigade routine - Drill Order, and Marching Order inspections, cleaning up generally including refitting and re-equiping.	
	2Ist		Hd-Qrs, "A"/88, "B"/88 & "D"/88 Batteries marched via LA CAUDESCURE - VIEUX BERQUIN - STRAZEELE to MERRIS where billets were taken.	
	22nd to 3Ist		Ordinary Brigade routine as from the I2th to the 20th carried out.	

[signature] Lieut: Col: R.F.A.

Commanding 88th Brigade R.F.A.

D. D. & L., London, E.C. (A8001) Wt. W1771/M2031 750,000 5/17 Sch. 52 Forms/C2118/14

Instructions regarding War Diaries and Intelligence Summaries are contained in F. S. Regs., Part II. and the Staff Manual respectively. Title pages will be prepared in manuscript.

WAR DIARY
or
INTELLIGENCE SUMMARY.
(Erase heading not required.)

Army Form C. 2118.

88 Bde R.F.A.
Vol 26

Place	Date	Hour	Summary of Events and Information	Remarks and references to Appendices
MERRIS	SEPTEMBER. 1st - 4th		Ordinary Brigade Routine carried out, including cleaning up and re-equipping.	Ref: Sheet 36 A 1/4000
	5th		1 section of each Battery (less "C"/88 Battery) relieved sections of 28th A.F.A. Brigade in action as follows:- "A"/88 O 3 c 6 4, "B"/88 O 3 a 1 1., "D"/88 O 3 d 3 5.	28 S.W. 1/20,000
SIEGE FARM N 16 c 2 9	6th		Remaining sections of batteries completed relief of 28th A.F.A. Bde: and Headquarters established at SIEGE FARM N 16 c 2 9 -(H.Q. 28th A.F.A. Bde: were taken over by 87th Bde: R.F.A.) and wagon line were taken over in N 5 c. "A"/88, "B"/88 and "D"/88 came under orders of 87th Brigade R.F.A. and with "A"/87 in action at O 2 b 7 4 formed the CANAL GROUP.	
	~~xxxx~~ 7th		Work commenced on 12 additional gun positions in areas O 9 a, O 3, I 33 d and O 2 b in connection with forthcoming offensive. Arrangements for Battle O.P.s and other tactical arrangements were also commenced.	
	8th - 11th		The above work continued and completed.	
	12th		During the evening 18th A.F.A. Bde: moved up into action to positions already prepared for them and came under the orders of H.Q. 88th Brigade R.F.A.	
	13th		During the evening 28th A.F.A. Bde: moved up into action to positions already prepared for them and came under the orders of H.Q. 88th Brigade R.F.A. now known as Hd-Qrs RIGHT ARTILLERY GROUP consisting of three sub-groups "A", "B" & "C".	
	14th		During the days registrations in new sub-group zones were carried out, and throughout the night harassing fire was brought to bear on targets which had been engaged by the heavies during the day.	
	15th		At 8.0 a.m. all batteries took part in "Corps Barrage No: 1" and further registrations carried out during the day. Night firing tasks laid down in Instructions for Offensive carried out.	
	16th		At 10.0 a.m an Army practice barrage (No: 1) was carried out in which all batteries of the Right Arty: Group took part. in addition to the ordinary day firing. Night firing programme carried out.	
	17th - 19th		During these days ~~xxxxxx~~ the usual day firing tasks were carried out, and in addition 3 Corps Barrages and 2 Army Barrages were taken part in. Night firing tasks as laid down were engaged each night. Hostile artillery was very active against the areas of battery positions during this time. Gas bombardments were also carried out.	
	20th		This being "Attack Day" and Zero hour 5.40 A.M., at that hour batteries opened out on the programme arranged in conjunction with the Infantry operations and continued this fire until conclusion of the operations	

D. D. & L., London, E.C.
(A8001) Wt. W1771/M2031 750,000 5/17 Sch. 52 Forms/C2118/14

Instructions regarding War Diaries and Intelligence Summaries are contained in F. S. Regs., Part II. and the Staff Manual respectively. Title pages will be prepared in manuscript.

WAR DIARY
or
INTELLIGENCE SUMMARY.
(Erase heading not required.)

Army Form C. 2118.

Place	Date	Hour	Summary of Events and Information	Remarks and references to Appendices
SIEGE FARM.	SEPTEMBER			
	20th (contd:)		During the remainder of the day reported concentrations of enemy troops were engaged and at 7.20 pm and S.O.S. Call by Infantry was responded to. During the night enemy communications, roads, tracks and bridges were kept under fire.	
	21st		At 4.30 a.m all batteries opened fire on their new S.O.S. Lines and searcher forward in lifts of 100 yds up to a range of 6200 yds. This fire continued until 5.15 a.m. At 7.10 pm an S.O.S Call was received and responded to. During the night harassing fire was carried out in Group zone. 18th A.F.A. Bde: withdrew from action to wagon lines and Group zone was re-adjusted accordingly.	
	22nd		During the day hostile artillery was very active against the area of battery positions and in the evening enemy aeroplanes crossed our lines and dropped bombs on various points. Night firing programme carried out.	
	23rd		During the day batteries engaged Dug-outs & tracks P 2 d 8 4, P 8 a 3½ 8½., and trenches in P 2 c. and at 5.30 pm another Corps Barrage was taken part in. The usual tasks were engaged throughout the night. Hostile artillery was again active against the area O 3 A and B and it appears that all the fire comes from direction of TENBRIELEN and WERVICQ.	
	24th		In the morning enemy communications were engaged and registration carried out. At 9.0 pm another Corps Barrage was taken part in. Night tasks carried out.	
	25th		Two practice barrages were taken part in, one at 6.30 a.m. and another at 2.0 p.m. Hostile artillery was again very active against battery positions and also his aeroplanes during the morning. From5.0 pm - 7.45 pm a gas bombardment was carried out by us against J 33 a. Night firing programme carried out.	
	26th		At 5.50 a.m. a smoke barrage was put up in conjunction with Infantry operations on our left. At 6.50 pm a "S.O.S." Call was received and reponded to. Harassing fire on roads, tracks and selected objectives was carried out during the night.	
	27th		At 5.0 a.m all batteries of the Group opened fire on "S.O.S" Lines and crept forward in lifts of 100 yds until a range of 6000 yds was reached; 4.5" Hows: ceasing fire at 5.51 am and 18-pounders at 5.33 a.m. At 5.0 pm a re-grouping of the Artillery took place and RIGHT ARTILLERY GROUP now consisted on 87th and 88th Brigades. Night firing tasks were engaged.	
	28th		At 2.0 a.m fire was brought to bear on O 6 d 6 2 where enemy were reported in shell-holes. Registration was carried out during the day. "C"/88 Battery having rejoined the Brigade from 2nd Army Arty: School took over from "A"/88 together with guns & equipment. "A"/88 Battery withdrew to its wagon line.	

D. D. & L., London, E.C.
(A8001) Wt. W1771/M2031 750,000 5/17 Sch. 52 Forms/C2118/14

Army Form C. 2118.

WAR DIARY
or
INTELLIGENCE SUMMARY.
(*Erase heading not required.*)

Instructions regarding War Diaries and Intelligence Summaries are contained in F. S. Regs., Part II. and the Staff Manual respectively. Title pages will be prepared in manuscript.

Place	Date	Hour	Summary of Events and Information	Remarks and references to Appendices
SIEGE FARM.	SEPTEMBER. 29th		Following targets were engaged by batteries during the day:- KIKI FARM, Occupied shell-holes in P 8 a and c, Dug-outs in O 2 b and roads and tracks in O 2 a. Hostile artillery was less active than usual during the day, although still active at night. Hostile aircraft was very active between 8.0 - 9.30 pm and dropped several bombs in the locality of VOORMEZEELE. Roads, tracks, dug-outs and selectex objectives were engaged throughout the night.	
	30th		Quiet day. A few registrations were carried out. Usual night firing carried out.	

[illegible signature] Major R.F.A.
Commanding 88th Brigade, R.F.A.

D. D. & L., London, E.C. (A8001) Wt. W1771/M2031 750,000 5/17 Sch. 52 Forms/C2118/14

19

88 Bde R G A
Vol 27

Instructions regarding War Diaries and Intelligence Summaries are contained in F. S. Regs., Part II, and the Staff Manual respectively. Title pages will be prepared in manuscript.

WAR DIARY
or
INTELLIGENCE SUMMARY.
(Erase heading not required.)

Army Form C. 2118.

Place	Date	Hour	Summary of Events and Information	Remarks and references to Appendices
SIEGE FARM N 16 c 2.9	1917 OCTOBER 1st		At 5.30 am an S.O.S. call was received & responded to. At 9.30 a.m. all batteries of the Group took part in an Army Practice Barrage (No 1). Remainder of day quiet except for enemy gas shelling of O.3.a. At 8.15 pm all batteries again took part in "Army Barrage No 2." Throughout night roads, tracks & selected objectives with Group Zone were kept under bursts of fire.	HOLLEBEKE 1/10.000 WYTSCHAETE 1/10.000.
	2nd		Quiet day. At 9.30 pm two hostile aeroplanes attacked B/88 position with Machine Gun fire. No casualties occasioned. The usual night firing was carried out.	
	3rd		Quiet day. Night firing programme carried out.	
	4th		At 6.0 am a barrage was put up by us, including a smoke screen, in conjunction with attack by 37th Division, fire ceasing at 7.30 am. ALASKA HOUSES & JAEGER TRENCH were engaged during the day by 4.5" hows. Remainder of day quiet on both sides. Night firing carried out. At 10 pm all batteries fired in barrage till 10.17 pm with silent periods in accordance with "Instructions for the Offensive."	
	5th		At 5.15 pm batteries took part in a further Preparatory Barrage. Few registrations carried out during day. Hostile artillery quiet. Further barrage taken part in from 11 pm – 11.17 pm. Usual harassing fire during night.	
	6th		No firing during day. Hostile artillery active about O.2 and O.3 during afternoon. Night firing [illegible] carried out.	

(A7383) Wt W593/M672 350,000 1/17 Sch. 52a Forms/C/2118/14

Instructions regarding War Diaries and Intelligence Summaries are contained in F. S. Regs., Part II, and the Staff Manual respectively. Title pages will be prepared in manuscript.

WAR DIARY
or
INTELLIGENCE SUMMARY.
(Erase heading not required.)

Army Form C. 2118.

Place	Date	Hour	Summary of Events and Information	Remarks and references to Appendices
SIEGE FARM N16c 2.9	1917 October 7th		No firing during day. Hostile artillery active about ST. ELOI X Roads. At 8pm batteries participated in "IX Corps Barrage No 1" until 8.24pm. Night firing carried out.	HOLLEBEKE 1/10.000 WYTSCHAETE 1/10.000
	8th		At 7.0 am batteries took part in "IX Corps Barrage No 2" until 7.30 am. Quiet day. "IX Corps Barrage No 3" took place from 11pm – 11.27pm. Usual harassing fire during night.	
	9th		At 5.20 am barrage & smoke screen were put up in support of attack by Corps on our left. Remainder of day quiet. Night firing carried out on enemy communications.	
	10th		At 4.25 am batteries took part in an Army Barrage. A few registrations carried out during day by balloon. Hostile artillery normal. Night firing carried out.	
	11th		At 5.0 am batteries took part in another Army Barrage. Hostile artillery was active around the area of Battery positions and CANAL BANK. Considerable aerial activity. Two hostile aeroplanes were brought down & one of ours crashed. Night firing carried out.	
	12th		Barrage at 5.25 am was taken part in. Hostile artillery very active throughout day especially about CANAL Bank & area O3. This fire was directed by hostile ~~balloon~~ aeroplane observation. At 10pm batteries took part in a further Retaliation Barrage. Night firing programme carried out.	
	13th		At 5.15 am a barrage was carried out as for yesterday morning. Quiet day. Night firing carried out.	

D. D. & L., London, E.C. (A7883) Wt W809/M1672 350,000 4/17 Sch. 52a Forms/C/2118/14

Army Form C. 2118.

Instructions regarding War Diaries and Intelligence Summaries are contained in F. S. Regs., Part II, and the Staff Manual respectively. Title pages will be prepared in manuscript.

WAR DIARY
or
INTELLIGENCE SUMMARY.
(Erase heading not required.)

Place	Date	Hour	Summary of Events and Information	Remarks and references to Appendices
SIEGE FARM N 16 c 2 9	1917 October 14th		Owing to re-grouping of 19th Div. Arty A/88 moved into action at I 34 c 95.05. D/88 moved to I 33 d 95.90 & came under orders of 87th Brigade R.F.A. (Left Group). Right Group now consists of A/28 in action at O 3 a 6 0, B/87 at O 3 a 4.2, C/87 at O 3 a 3.4, B/88 at O 3 a 1.1, C/88 at O 3 c 6.4 and 65th Battery at O 2 d 7.7. Group zone unaltered. Registration of new zero point carried out by batteries. Enemy aircraft very active, one enemy plane being driven down by A.A. fire. Night firing carried out.	HOLLEBEKE 1/10.000 WYTSCHAETE 1/10.000
	15th		Enemy artillery ~~[illegible]~~ fairly active all day, O 3 being under fire almost all day. Night harassing fire carried out. Enemy aeroplanes flew low over HOLLEBEKE during afternoon.	
	16th		Enemy artillery extremely active throughout day on O.3, CANAL Bank & I 33 a & b. Many batteries were observed engaged by our counter-batteries. We carried out usual night firing.	
	17th		Between 11.40 am & 3 pm C/88 engaged farms P 9 c 2½.7 with incendiary shells with excellent results. Enemy artillery very active against O 3 a & c all day. Night firing carried out.	
	18th		Fairly quiet day. A good deal of aerial activity. Night firing as usual. During evening enemy dropped bombs in the vicinity of THE MOUND.	
	19th		Quiet day. In addition to usual night tasks ~~[illegible]~~ 65th engaged ALASKA HOUSES with gas shell from 7.30 pm to 10.30 pm	

D. D. & L., London, E.C. (A7859) Wt W809/M1672 350,000 4/17 Sch. 52a Forms/C/2118/14

Instructions regarding War Diaries and Intelligence Summaries are contained in F. S. Regs., Part II. and the Staff Manual respectively. Title pages will be prepared in manuscript.

WAR DIARY
or
INTELLIGENCE SUMMARY.
(Erase heading not required.)

Army Form C. 2118.

Place	Date	Hour	Summary of Events and Information	Remarks and references to Appendices
SIEGE FARM	1917 OCTOBER			HOLLEBEKE
N16c29	20th		No day firing. Enemy artillery + aircraft below normal. Night firing programme carried out.	1/10 000
	21st.		Registration carried out. During afternoon 65th Battery engaged ALASKA HOUSES with gas shells.	WYTSCHAETE
			Enemy artillery quiet, but aircraft active during morning. At 5.45 pm enemy dropped	1/10 000
			bombs in KEMMEL. Night firing carried out; Owing to re constitution of 19th Div. ARTY the 88th Brigade is now only comprised of batteries 88th Bde. from 6 pm 21st.	
	22nd		At 5.30 a.m. batteries took part in "Army Barrage No 1". During morning, owing to mist we	
			engaged back areas in enemy lines. Usual harassing fire during night carried out.	
	23rd		Between 1 pm – 3.30 pm B/88 fired bursts of fire on roads + dug-outs. Enemy artillery extremely active	
			in I 33 c and I 34 d. Night programme carried out. At 8.15 pm batteries fired	
	~~24th~~		preparatory bursts of fire in accordance with instructions for the offensive.	
	24th		At 9.15 am batteries fired in "Army Barrage No 1" ceasing at 9.46 a.m. Registrations	
			carried out during afternoon. Night firing carried out. From 8.15 pm to 8.51 pm batteries	
			again fired preparatory bursts of fire as per programme.	
	25th		Registration carried out. Enemy artillery quiet. Harassing fire carried out throughout night.	
	~~26th~~		B/88 firing gas shell.	
	26th		At 5.40 a.m. batteries opened on barrage in support of attack on our left. D/88 firing	
			smoke + gas shell. During afternoon A/88 fired bursts on the Protective Barrage line.	
			Enemy extremely quiet. Night programme carried out.	

D. D. & L., London, E.C. (A7883) Wt. W803/M1672 350,000 4/17 Sch. 52a Forms/C/2118/14

Instructions regarding War Diaries and Intelligence Summaries are contained in F. S. Regs., Part II. and the Staff Manual respectively. Title pages will be prepared in manuscript.

WAR DIARY
or
INTELLIGENCE SUMMARY.
(*Erase heading not required.*)

Army Form C. 2118.

Place	Date	Hour	Summary of Events and Information	Remarks and references to Appendices
SIEGE FARM. N 16 c 2 9	27th		A few registrations carried out. Enemy aeroplanes attacked our balloons during morning causing occupants to descend. Our aircraft very active all day. Night firing programme carried out.	HOLLEBEKE 1/10.000 HYTSHAETE 1/10.000.
	[illegible]		Owing to personnel of 87th Brigade being withdrawn to wagon lines B/88 personnel took over guns in action of A/87 & A/88 took over guns of B/88 handing over its guns to A/87 at wagon lines. Zones re adjusted accordingly.	
	28th		No day firing. Enemy artillery normal. Night firing carried out.	
	29th		Registrations on PILL BOX P 2 d 6.8 carried out. Enemy very quiet. Enemy aeroplanes dropped bombs in area I 33 b & d. Night harassing fire carried out.	
	30th		From 5.50 to 6.20 a.m. batteries fired in barrage in support of attack on our left. D/88 firing smoke shell. Enemy did not reply to this & was fairly quiet all day. Night firing programme carried out.	
	31st		Registration on BASSEVILLE FARM & PILL BOX P2 d 6.8 carried out. Enemy artillery very quiet except for occasional burst against vicinity of gun positions. Night firing carried out.	

J.O. Campbell.
Major R.F.A.
Commanding 88th Brigade R.F.A.

D. D. & L., London, E.C.
(A7883) Wt. W803/M1672 350,000 4/17 Sch. 52a Forms/C/2118/14

88 Bde RFA
Vol 28

Army Form C. 2118.

Instructions regarding War Diaries and Intelligence Summaries are contained in F. S. Regs., Part II, and the Staff Manual respectively. Title pages will be prepared in manuscript.

WAR DIARY
or
INTELLIGENCE SUMMARY.
(Erase heading not required.)

Place	Date	Hour	Summary of Events and Information	Remarks and references to Appendices
SIEGE FARM N.16.c.2.9.	Nov 1st		Quiet day. During the afternoon there was a good deal of aerial activity on both sides. Between 8.20 and 9.10 pm all batteries took part in programme arranged to support an Infantry raid on dug-outs about J.26.d.75.55. Hostile artillery retaliation to this raid was nil. Night firing tasks were carried out during the night	Ref. HOLLEBEKE 1/10,000 & WYTSCHAETE 1/10,000
	2nd		Visibility poor throughout the day – little activity on either side. The usual night firing tasks were carried out throughout the night.	
	3rd		Hostile Aircraft were active during the morning directing hostile fire on RAVINE WOOD. These were engaged by the Lewis guns attached to Batteries. During the night the usual night firing tasks, including the use of gas shell were carried out	
	4th		A few registrations were carried out during the afternoon with good results. The enemy's artillery were active in the vicinity of the BLUFF & Canal Bank in O.3 & I.34.a	
	6th		At 6.0am all batteries took part in the programme arranged in conjunction with an attack made by the Canadian Corps. The attack was successful all objectives being gained. Hostile retaliation to our fire was very feeble only	

D. D. & L., London, E.C. (A7883) Wt. W803/M1672 350,000 4/17 Sch. 52a Forms/C2118/14

Army Form C. 2118.

Instructions regarding War Diaries and Intelligence Summaries are contained in F. S. Regs., Part II. and the Staff Manual respectively. Title pages will be prepared in manuscript.

WAR DIARY
or
INTELLIGENCE SUMMARY.
(Erase heading not required.)

Place	Date	Hour	Summary of Events and Information	Remarks and references to Appendices
SIEGE FARM. N.16c29.	6th		a few rounds 77mm being fired about I 33d & I 34b. Visibility was poor throughout the day. During the night the usual night firing tasks were carried out.	Maps HOLLEBEKE 1/20,000 & WYTSCHAETE 1/10,000
	7th		Registrations were carried out during the day. EAs were fairly active about 3.15 pm but they were driven off by our AA fire & the Lewis Guns attached to Batteries. Throughout the night hostile aircraft were unusually active bombing behind our lines – this continued until dawn.	
	8th		EAs again active during the morning and 5 machines were driven down by our aeroplanes & A.A. fire. Hostile Artillery was very quiet throughout the day.	
	9th		During the morning SPOIL BANK, CANAL BANK & Batteries in the vicinity were heavily shelled. This shoot was apparently directed by EAs as there were 15 up at the time.	
	10th		Quiet Day, very little activity on either side with artillery fire or aerial activity. Throughout the night selected targets within the Brigade zone were kept under intermittent bursts of fire.	
	11th		Slight hostile fire against I 33b otherwise a quiet day. During the night the 112th Infy. Brigade (37th Division) relieved the 89th Infy Bde (30th Division).	

D. D. & L., London, E.C. (A7883) Wt. W809/M1671 350,000 4/17 Sch. 52a Forms/C/2118/14

Instructions regarding War Diaries and Intelligence Summaries are contained in F. S. Regs., Part II. and the Staff Manual respectively. Title pages will be prepared in manuscript.

WAR DIARY or INTELLIGENCE SUMMARY.

(Erase heading not required.)

Army Form C. 2118.

Place	Date	Hour	Summary of Events and Information	Remarks and references to Appendices
SIEGE FARM. N.16c 29	12th		EAs were active during the morning & were engaged by our AA & Lewis guns, - one plane was driven down out of control in our lines. Registrations were carried out during the afternoon & selected targets kept under intermittent bursts of fire throughout the night.	HOLLEBEKE 1/10,000 & WYTSCHAETE 1/10,000
	13		Visibility poor throughout the day. Hostile artillery were very active between 10.50 and 11.50 am on squares I 33 b, c & d and I 34 c.	
	15th		Brigade Hd. Qrs moved from SIEGE FARM to LOCK 7 (I.32 b. 7.3). At about 11.0am an E.A was brought down in flames & at 12.15 another plane (nationality unknown) was seen to fall in the enemys lines. A flight of 1 Gotha & 6 others were unsuccessfully engaged by our AA fire at 2.15 pm.	
	16th		Activity on both sides considerably below normal. Batteries moved their wagon lines back to the following position: A/88 M 21.c.1.7 & M 15c 5.2, B/88 X.6.a 6.4., C/88 R.35c.1.8., D/88 M.16c.3.8. The usual night firing tasks were carried out.	
	17th		Visibility bad. Hostile artillery nil. The usual night firing tasks carried out. During the afternoon & night the 112th Infy Brigade were relieved by the 111th Infy Bde	

D. D. & L., London, E.C. (A7883) Wt. W809/M1672 350,000 4/17 Sch. 52a Forms/C/2118/14

Instructions regarding War Diaries and Intelligence Summaries are contained in F. S. Regs., Part II, and the Staff Manual respectively. Title pages will be prepared in manuscript.

WAR DIARY
or
INTELLIGENCE SUMMARY.
(*Erase heading not required.*)

Army Form C. 2118.

Place	Date	Hour	Summary of Events and Information	Remarks and references to Appendices
				Maps:-
LOCK 7.	18th		During the day a few registrations were carried out by batteries. Hostile artillery were fairly active between 7am & 11am against the area I 33d 8.3 & I 33d 4.7.	HOLLEBEKE 1/10,000 & WYTSCHAETE 1/10,000
			At 8.15am an EA attacked & brought down one of our observation balloons in the vicinity of YPRES. This 'plane was engaged by our M.Gs but without success.	
			Hostile artillery were again active against I 33 b & d during the afternoon but soon ceased upon retaliation by our heavy artillery.	
	19th		Visibility poor & activity practically nil on both sides. Night firing tasks carried out	
	20		" " " " " " " " " " " "	
	21		Quiet during the morning but during the afternoon SPOIL BANK & vicinity came in for a good deal of shelling.	
	22		Hostile artillery considerably above normal throughout the day & flashes of several batteries observed. In addition to the usual night firing tasks, D/88 Battery carried out a Gas Shell bombardment.	
	23		At 1.30pm all batteries opened fire on their S.O.S. lines for test purposes. During the afternoon EAs were very active - about 18 being counted in the air over our forward area at the same time. From dusk until dawn they were	

D. D. & L., London, E.C.
(A7883) Wt. W803/M1672 350,000 4/17 Sch. 52a. Forms/C/2118/14

Instructions regarding War Diaries and Intelligence Summaries are contained in F. S. Regs., Part II. and the Staff Manual respectively. Title pages will be prepared in manuscript.

WAR DIARY
or
INTELLIGENCE SUMMARY.
(*Erase heading not required.*)

Army Form C. 2118.

Place	Date	Hour	Summary of Events and Information	Remarks and references to Appendices
				Appx
LOCK 4.	22"		again active & many bombs were dropped.	HOLLEBEKE & 1/10,000 &
	23"		Several registrations carried out during the morning. Hostile artillery active about Oila	WYTSCHAETE 1/10,000
			& Canal Bank but ceased upon retaliation by our heavy artillery.	
	25"		During the day reported 'centres of movement' within our zone were engaged & the night	
			firing tasks carried out. Hostile artillery were again active throughout the afternoon against	
			SPOIL BANK & Batteries in the vicinity.	
	26"		GAME COPSE, CHALK FARM & dug outs at P8a 30.85 & P.1.d. 20.65 were engaged	
			by our fire during the morning & a few registrations carried out. Hostile artillery quiet	
			only a few rounds of 10cm being fired about the vicinity of NORFOLK LODGE	
	26"		At 5.0 pm all batteries opened fire on the area J22d. 0.7 to 6.7. in addition to their	
			usual night firing tasks	
	27"		At 5.0am the concentration of fire of the previous evening was repeated against J28a & c.	
			apparently with good result as no movement was observed in the area throughout the day	
			Hostile artillery was also very quiet. The usual night firing tasks were carried out	
	28"		Harassing fire carried out on selected targets & reported centres of movement during the	
			day. Hostile Artillery were active during the morning about I 33c & about SPOIL BANK	

D. D. & L., London, E.C. (A7883) Wt. W803/M1672 350,000 4/17 Sch. 52a Forms/C/2118/14

Instructions regarding War Diaries and Intelligence Summaries are contained in F. S. Regs., Part II. and the Staff Manual respectively. Title pages will be prepared in manuscript.

WAR DIARY
or
INTELLIGENCE SUMMARY.
(Erase heading not required.)

Army Form C. 2118.

Place	Date	Hour	Summary of Events and Information	Remarks and references to Appendices
LOCK 7	28		between 7·0pm & 8·0pm. One of our observation balloons broke loose during the afternoon & drifted over the enemy's lines. One of our aeroplanes was also brought down by an EA in the neighbourhood of GHELUVELT. Selected targets were kept under intermittent bursts of fire throughout the night.	HOLLEBEKE MAP 1/10,000 + WYTSCHAETE 1/10,000
	29th		At 4·30 am another 'concentration' was carried out in conjunction with the remainder of the 37th Div: Arty: This was repeated at 4·45 pm. There was very little hostile fire during the day & visibility was bad. The usual night firing programme was carried out.	
	30th		Burst of fire were carried out on selected targets during the day. Hostile artillery was considerably below normal.	

[signature]
Captain R.F.A
Adjutant 88th Brigade R.F.A.

D. D. & L., London, E.C.
(A7883) Wt. W803/M1672 350,000 4/17 Sch. 52a Forms/C/2118/14

Instructions regarding War Diaries and Intelligence Summaries are contained in F. S. Regs., Part II. and the Staff Manual respectively. Title pages will be prepared in manuscript.

WAR DIARY
or
INTELLIGENCE SUMMARY.
(Erase heading not required.)

Army Form C. 2118.

Vol 29

Place	Date	Hour	Summary of Events and Information	Remarks and references to Appendices
LOCK 7 I 32 b 7 3	1917 DECEMBER			HOLLEBEKE 1/10,000 Special Map No: 8120 1/10,000
		1st	Day firing on selected targets was carried out, and in connection with a forthcoming operation by Corps on left, concentrations were carried out by D/88 Battery at 6.30 a.m., at 11.45 a.m by all batteries, 7.0 - 7.25 pm by A/88, B/88 & D/88, and at 6.30 pm, 9.30 pm & 12.15 am by all batteries. Enemy artillery inactive, both during day and night.	
		2nd	Another concentration was carried out by B/88 and D/88 at 5.30 a.m. During the day selected targets were engaged. Hostile artillery active against CANAL BANK. MOLEN ROAD and THE BLUFF during day. Night firing programme carried out on enemy communications. roads & tracks.	
		3rd	From 12 Noon to 2.0 pm B/88 and D/88 carried out programme in conjunction with operations by Corps on our left. D/88 firing smoke shell. Other selected targets were engaged by batteries during the day. Enemy artillery again active against THE BLUFF and about 40 rounds 77mm were directed against Brigade O.P. at O 11 a 25 40. During night enemy shelled SPOIL BANK, I 32 b. & I 33 b with gas shell. Night firing tasks were carried out. Enemy dropped many bombs in the back areas during the night.	
		4th	Selected targets engaged during the day and registration. Enemy artillery normal except against area O 5 a and c. A few enemy aeroplanes flew over our sector during the morning but were driven off by A.A. fire. Night firing carried out.	
		5th	Usual day firing on selected targets including KIKI FARM and PILL BOX P 2 d 6 8, registration and calibration. Hostile artillery lightly engaged O 11 a. SPOIL BANK, CANAL BANK, O 2 a and OAF AVENUE in O 5 c. E.A. were active flying over battery areas at 8.15 am and 1.30 pm. Night firing tasks carried out.	
		6th	Bursts of fire on selected targets carried out during day. Enemy artillery considerably above normal, shelling roads & tracks from 8 am - 10 am with H.V. guns, and SPOIL BANK & THE BLUFF throughout the day. E.A. active during the morning, and between 5.30 - 6 pm several dropped bombs in our lines - at 5.40 pm one of these planes was brought down. Usual night firing.	
		7th	Enemy artillery active against SPOIL BANK and I 33 d-shoot on SPOIL BANK being directed by aeroplane. At 4.45 pm D/88 Battery carried out a shoot on VORSTRAAT CABARET with 166 rounds gas shell and from 5.15 pm to 12 mn special night firing carried out in view of suspected enemy relief.	
		8th	Registration carried out on P 2 d 6 8 and selected targets engaged. Enemy artillery showed marked activity in the afternoon against I 33 d and I 34 c. E.A. active during day. Night firing as usual. Enemy arty: engaged O 3 C, SPOIL BANK and I 32 b during the night.	

D. D. & L., London, E.C.
(A8001) Wt. W1771/M2031 750,000 5/17 Sch. 52 Forms/C2118/14

Instructions regarding War Diaries and Intelligence Summaries are contained in F. S. Regs., Part II. and the Staff Manual respectively. Title pages will be prepared in manuscript.

WAR DIARY
or
INTELLIGENCE SUMMARY.

(Erase heading not required.)

Army Form C. 2118.

Place	Date 1917 DECEMBER.	Hour	Summary of Events and Information	Remarks and references to Appendices
LOCK 7. I 32 b 7 3	9th		Dug-out P 13 a 54 68, PILL BOX P 2 d 6 8, KIKI FARM and other targets engaged during the day. Enemy artillery slightly active during the night in I 34 b, SPOIL BANK and THE BLUFF. Night firing programme carried out.	HOLLEBEKE 1/10,000
	10th		Calibration was carried out with salvaged ammunition during the day. Enemy artillery very active against THE BLUFF. At 12.20 p.m. 10 GOTHAS crossed our lines and some bombs were dropped. 7 others crossed our lines at 2.45 pm and carried out reconnaissances. ~~Xxxxxxxxxxxxxxxxxx~~ ~~xxxx~~ At 10.0 pm and 1.0 a.m enemy heavily shelled our forward area which ceased on special rockets being sent up by the enemy. Night firing on suspected H.Q., PIE FARM, R.E. Dump at P 7 a 8 5 and M.G. emplacement P 1 b 8 4.	Special Map No: 8120 d. 1/10,000 ZILLEBEKE 1/10,000
	11th		Suspected H.Q. in P 3 a, b & d, dug-outs in P 3 c and other selected targets engaged during day. Enemy artillery inactive, but engaged THE BLUFF, I 32 b and I 34 a and c during the evening.	28 S.W. 1/20,000
	12th		At 5.15 a.m enemy put up a barrage on our Right Centre Battalion front. Selected targets engaged and calibration carried out. Enemy artillery active against SPOIL BANK and I 33 d. At 2.15 pm about 15 GOTHAS flew over our lines and some bombs were dropped. Special night firing programme on roads, tracks, dug-outs etc. in view of suspected enemy relief.	Sheet 28 1/40,000
	13th		Tracks in P 8 a & P 2 d, KIKI FARM, P 3 d 52 70 and other targets engaged during day. Enemy artillery unusually inactive all day. An enemy patrol of 5 aeroplanes were active at 11.30 a.m. flying along our lines from South to North. Night firing carried out.	
N 7 a 7 8	14th		During the evening Batteries withdrew to their wagon lines, A/88, B/88 & D/88 withdrawing their guns, C/88 withdrawing guns of C/123 Battery (37th Div:). C/123 taking over positions and guns of C/88. Headquarters ~~xxxxxxxxxxxxxx~~ relieved by H.Q. 123rd Brigade who took over Command of Right Group 37th Divl. Arty. Headquarters established at N 7 a 7 8.	
	15th		One Section per battery relieved one section of corresponding batteries 148th Brigade R.F.A in positions as follows:- A/88 relieved A/148 at I 18 b 97 75, B/88 relieved B/148 at I 18 b 7 1, C/88 relieved C/148 at I 23 b 65 40, D/88 relieved D/148 at I 23 b 00 30. Reliefs of personnel only guns being exchanged complete.	
	16th		Relief of remaining two Sections per battery completed and Batteries 88th Brigade R.F.A now come under the Command of 149th Brigade R.F.A. who, with batteries 149th Bde: form NORTHERN GROUP 30th Divl. Artillery. Headquarters 88th Brigade remain at N 7 a 7 8. Wagon lines moved to:- A/88 to M 25 c 3 4, B/88 to M 34 c 8 7, C/88 to R 35 c 2 8, D/88 to N 2 a 8 8.	
	~~xxxx~~ 17th 18th		Batteries 88th Brigade R.F.A. under tactical orders of 30th Divl. Artillery. H.Q. still at N 7 a 7 8	

D. D. & L., London, E.C. (A5001) Wt. W1771/M2031 750,000 5/17 Sch. 52 Forms/C2118/14

Army Form C. 2118.

WAR DIARY
or
INTELLIGENCE SUMMARY.

(Erase heading not required.)

Instructions regarding War Diaries and Intelligence Summaries are contained in F. S. Regs., Part II. and the Staff Manual respectively. Title pages will be prepared in manuscript.

Place	Date	Hour	Summary of Events and Information	Remarks and references to Appendices
N 7 a 7 8	1917 DECEMBER			Sheet 28 SW 1/20,000 Sheet 28 1/40,000 Sheet 57 c 1/40,000
	19th) 20th) 21st)		Batteries 88th Bde: under tactical orders of 30th D.A. H.Q/88 remain at N 7 a 7 8 During morning of 21st B/88 wagon line moved to WARBURG Camp "A" at H 32 c 99 20.	
G 36 a 7 8	22nd		" " " " " " " . Headquarters moved to G 36 a 7 8.	
	23rd) 24th) 25th)		" " " " " " " . Headquarters still at G 36 a 7 8.	
	26th		1 Section per battery were relieved by batteries of the 20th Divl. Artillery. Reliefs of personnel only. guns being exchanged.	
	27th		Remaining Sections of batteries relieved and relief completed. Batteries 88th Brigade now at Wagon Lines.	
	28th) 29th)		Ordinary Brigade Routine, and preparations made for move to Third Army Area.	
	30th		Batteries entrained at BAILLEUL (West) Station for BAPAUME at the following times. A/88 at 11.18 a.m., B/88 at 3.28 p.m., C/88 at 7.18 p.m., D/88 at 11.18 p.m. Upon detraining during Night 30th and morning of 31st Batteries marched to ROCQUIGNY and camped in Camp "B".	
	31st		Brigade H.Q. entrained at 3.28 a.m. and on arrival at BAPAUME also marched to "B" Camp at ROCQUIGNY.	

[signature]
Lieutenant Colonel, R.F.A
Commanding 88th Brigade, R.F.A.

D. D. & L., London, E.C.
(A8001) Wt. W1771/M2031 750,000 5/17 Sch. 52 Forms/C2118/14

Instructions regarding War Diaries and Intelligence Summaries are contained in F. S. Regs., Part II. and the Staff Manual respectively. Title pages will be prepared in manuscript.

WAR DIARY
or
INTELLIGENCE SUMMARY.

(Erase heading not required.)

Army Form C. 2118.

88 Bde R.F.A. Vol 30

Place	Date	Hour	Summary of Events and Information	Remarks and references to Appendices
CAMP "B" ROCQUIGNY	1918 January	Ist	Ordinary Brigade Routine. Preparations made for move of Battery wagon lines.	57 c I/40000
	"	2nd	Battery wagon lines moved via BUS - YTRES - NEUVILLE to wagon lines about ROYAULCOURT. Approximate locations of same A/88, C/88 and D/88 on N. side of road at P.I7.a.2.8. and "B/88" about P I8 a 4 4. One Section of each Battery relieved corresponding batteries of 79th A.F.A. Brigade as follows A/88 relieved A/89 at K.36.c.05 35, B/88 at (4 guns) K 34 b 95 55 (2 guns) K 29 c 00 I7, C/88 at K 34 b 75 95, D/88 at (5 hows:) K 34 b 95 45 (I How:) K 30 c 80 75. Personnel only relieved, guns sights etc. being exchanged.	
K 36 a 6 0	"	3rd	Relief of Batteries 79th Brigade completed. Hd-Qrs 88th Brigade took over from H.Q. 79th A.F.A. Brigade at K 36 a 6 0 and relief now being completed, H.Q. 88th Bde: with A/155 at K.35.a.I2.I3 and C/155 at K 35 d 9 7 formed the Left Artillery Group. Night firing carried out on CANTAING VILLAGE, CANTAING SUPPORT TRENCH, tracks and communications within the Group Zone.	57.C. N.E.4 I/10000
	"	4th	Between 6.30am and 7.0am and between I0.0am and I2 noon Hostile Artillery was very active shelling the HINDENBURG LINE & Area in K 36 also K 29d and K 23 c. Enemy Aircraft very active throughout the day in reconnaissance and dropping bombs. Night firing tasks carried out on suitabe objectives throughout the night.	
	"	5th	Quiet day. Night firing tasks carried out. (Note:) Forthe purposes of night firing a single gun is run forward each night to a position already selected, carries out its programme arranged and is withdrawn to the Battery position before dawn.	
	"	8th	At 9.0am the Left Arty: Group zone was extended to cover the front of the Left Infantry Bde: viz:- from L 34 a 5 2 to L 2I c 8 4, and reconstituted as follows:- A/87, B/88, D/88, "A", "B", "C" & "D" Batteries 232 A.F.A. Bde:	
	"	9th	Roads andtracks searched by A/232 between 6 and 7.0am. Hostile Artillery active against L 25 d 5 5 and vicinity between II.30 and I2.15pm. E.As active over Battery areas. During the night Hd-Qrs at L 23 a 80 99, Cross Roads etc, and special firing on roads, tracks etc within group zone carried out, with a view of suspected enemy relief.	
	"	10th	Registrations and Calibrations carried out also movement in L I6 d and L 22 b. E.As were active during the morning over Battery areas. From 8.5I to 8.53pm all batteries fired on their S.O.S. lines in response to an S.O.S. Signal. Night firing tasks carried out. "A"/88 Battery took over from C/87th Battery I gun at L 26 d 9.3. in exchange for I of their own. This gun only being used for "Anti-Tank" defence only.	
	"	IIth	From 6.I7 to 6.45am all Batteries opened fire on their S.O.S. lines and searched back in view of a possible concentration by the enemy.	

D. D. & L., London, E.C. (A8001) Wt. W1771/M2031 750,000 5/17 Sch. 52 Forms/C2118/14

Instructions regarding War Diaries and Intelligence Summaries are contained in F. S. Regs., Part II. and the Staff Manual respectively. Title pages will be prepared in manuscript.

WAR DIARY
or
INTELLIGENCE SUMMARY.
(Erase heading not required.)

Army Form C. 2118.

Place	Date	Hour	Summary of Events and Information	Remarks and references to Appendices
K 36 a 6 0	Jan:	IIth	During the day registrations and aggressive shooting on Suspected H.Qs, tracks etc carried out. Enemy rather active against RIBECOURT & FLESQUIERES. Night firing on enemy posts, M.Gs. Road junctions etc. carried out.	57 C N.E.4. I/40000.
	"	I2th	At 9.30am and II.0am Hostile Batteries at L II b 5 3 and L II b 0 32 respectively were reported active and engaged. Registrations carried out and movement in MARCOING engaged. Enemy artillery and aircraft very active, MOLE TRENCH and K 36 a and b being heavily shelled. Night firing tasks carried out and road from chalk pit at L I6 c 2 6 being engaged by the sniping gun.	
	"	I3th	Marked increase in Hostile Artillery fire K.36, BOAR VALLET, RIBECOURT and Q I2 a being heavily shelled. E.As. were very active throughout the day registering flying low over targets. One of our observations balloons was brought down at 3.30pm by E.As. At 4.30pm the Group again re-organized (The 232 A.F.A. Bde: leaving the Group and B/88 & C/87 joining thegroup) Battery zones adjusted accordingly.	
	"	I4th	At II.30am A/87 Battery dispersed carrying party at L I6 b 9 I. Enemy much less active. Night firing tasks carried out:Bridges over CANAL DE ST QUENTIN being engaged by sniping gun.	
	"	I5th	Registrations, movement on road L I6 c 9 5 engaged . Enemy Artillery very quiet. "D"/87 Battery come under orders of the Group.	
	"	I6th	Movement in L I6 c and d engaged. From 3.30pm to 4.0pm the enemy put up a concentrated gas bombardment (200 rds) on L 24.d.5x8. otherwise quiet. Night firing tasks carried out.	
	"	I7th	Movement in MARCOING COPSE and road L I6 d 3 5 to L I6 c 65 50 engaged, also suspected forward guns in L 23 d. In view of suspected enemy relief all roads and tracks in L 35, L 29 c and L 34 b were kept under intermittent bursts of fire from 8.0pm to I2 midnight. Ordinary night firing tasks also carried out.	
	"	I8th	Movement in R.5.a. and L 35 c engaged. Enemy artillery very active throughtout the morning BOAR COPSE, L 3I d and L 32 C being heavily shelled. E.As were active during the morning carrying out registrations. Usual night firing tasks carried out.	
	"	I9th	Registrations and calibrations carried out, movement in L I6 d and c. and L 34 b & c engaged and dispersed. In retaliation for hostile shelling MARCOING COPSE, Roads in L 29 a &b and L 28 b 5 6 were engaged by all batteries from 3.30pm and 4.0pm. E.As very active during early morning.	
	"	20th	MARCOING COPSE engaged and movement on road through L I6 c and d, L 34 b 4 2 and L 28 b5 6 dispersed. Hostile artillery active during the day against K 35 b and BOAR COPSE. E.As were active between I0.0am and I2 noon directing hostile fire, The usual night firing tasks carried out.	

D. D. & L., London, E.C. (A8001) Wt. W1771/M1031 750,000 5/17 Sch. 52 Forms/C2118/14

Instructions regarding War Diaries and Intelligence Summaries are contained in F. S. Regs., Part II. and the Staff Manual respectively. Title pages will be prepared in manuscript.

WAR DIARY
or
INTELLIGENCE SUMMARY.

(Erase heading not required.)

Army Form C. 2118.

Place	Date	Hour	Summary of Events and Information	Remarks and references to Appendices
K 36 a 6 0	Jan	21st	Movement observed and engaged in L 29 d and L I6 a. Hostile Aircraft active throughout morning apparently directing shoot on K 36 c 5 5. Usual Night firi ng tasks carried out.	
	"	22nd	At 2.0pm the Group again re constructed, "C"/87 and "D"/87 Batteries being transferred from the Group and "C"/88th Battery into the Group.	
	"	23rd	Enemy Artillery very active during the afternoon against RIBECOURT and road to TRESCAULT. At 4.45pm all batteries retaliated on their S.O.S. lines and searching back for 3 minutes. This was apparently succesful as little hostile fire took place afterwards. Night firing tasks carried out, with special attention paid to tracks and communicat ion trenches within zone in view of suspected enemy relief.	
	"	24th	Registrations carried out and suspected forward gun atL 23 d engaged. Visibility very poor. The usual night firing tasks carried out throughout night.	
	"	25th	Hostile aircraft very active ofer forward and battery areas throughout the morning. A suspected Trench Mortar at L 28 c 7 3 and movement in L 22 c was engaged by our fire. Except for about I00 rounds 77 mm which fell about L 27 c. hostile artillery were quiet.	
	"	26th	E.As. were very active throughout the day registering and reconnoitring. In the evening and during the night they were also active bombing back areas in the neighbourhood of HAVRINGCOURT WOOD.	
	"	27th	Quiet day. A thick mist rendered all observation impossible. Between II.0pm and 2.0am COUILLET VALLEY R.2.d. and HIGHLAND RIDGE bombarded with gas shell.	
	"	28th	From 9.0am to I2 noon E.As. were very active over forward areas. I.E.A. was brought down by our Lewis gun fire. Individual movement was engaged in L I6 c during the morning. E.As were also active during the night dropping bombs in back areas.	
	"	29th	Hostile artillery very aggressive against the area Q 5 & 6 and K 35 (5% gas shell)	
	"	30th	Bursts of fire maintained on enemy communications etc. within Group zone. Hostile Arty: quiet. A heavy mist prevented observation.	
	"	3Ist	New work at L 22 c 9 5, Post at L 23 c I 9, New trench at L 28 c 6 9 and track from L I6 c 8 5 to L I6 c 6 0 were engaged during the day by our fire. Hostile Artillery was active against WAR COPSE and TRESCAULT RIBECOURT Road; the shoot being conducted with aeroplane observation. During the afternoon one enemy balloon was driven down by one of our aeroplanes.	

[signature] Capt for Major R.F.A.
Commanding 88th: Brigade R.F.A.

D. D. & L., London, E.C. (A8001) Wt. W1771/M2031 750,000 5/17 Sch. 52 Forms/C2118/14

Instructions regarding War Diaries and Intelligence Summaries are contained in F. S. Regs., Part II. and the Staff Manual respectively. Title pages will be prepared in manuscript.

WAR DIARY
or
INTELLIGENCE SUMMARY.

(*Erase heading not required.*)

Army Form C. 2118.

88 Bde R.G.A.
Vol 31

Place	Date	Hour	Summary of Events and Information	Remarks and references to Appendices
K 36 a 6 0	February Ist I918.		Owing to thick mist observation was impossible. Harrassing fire was directed against, roads and tracks within the group zone by all Batteries of the Group from IO.Oam to 4.Opm. Hostile Artillery was very quiet throughout the day. During the night the usual night firing tasks were carried out, special attention being given to road running through NOYELLES by the sniping gun.	Sheet 57 C NE. I/IOOOO
	2nd.		Individual movement was observed and engaged between MARCOING & NINE WOOD. Machine guns at L 22 c 85 25 & L 28 d I 5 I5 and new work at L 22 ~~xxx~~ a O 5 were also engaged during the day. Enemy Aircraft were very active during the morning over our forward system but retired under our A.A. fire. Throughout the night the usual night firing tasks were carried out.	
	3rd.		Very quiet on both sides throughout the day. At 5.Opm all Batteries bombarded suspected Hd-Qrs in MARCOING for 3 minutes. Night firing tasks carried out.	
	4th		Registrations carried out, and movement in MARCOING engaged. From I2.30 to I.30am hostile artillery were very active against the Area K 36 a and b and Q 6 c 5 5. The usual Night firing tasks were carried out.	
	5th		At 6.Oam to 6.I5 am all Batteries opened fire on their S.O.S. lines and searched back, paying special attention to likely points where enemy would assemble for an attack. Hostile arty: were fairly active during the afternoon in the vicinity of Q.5.a. and b. & BOAR COPSE. Enemy Aircraft much below normal.	
	6th		Movement was observed and engaged in L 23 d during the morning and registrations carried out. Hostile artillery very active against TRESCAULT - RIBECOURT Road from 5.30 to 7.Opm	
	7th		Enemy Artillery fairly active against TRESCAULT - RIBECOURT Road during the evening otherwise activity on both sides Nil. Night firing tasks carried out.	
	8th to IOth		Except for night firing tasks carried out each night there was very little activity on either side, during this period.	
	IIth		Considerable individual movement was observed during the morning in L I6 central and engaged. From 2.Opm to 2.30pm the enemy became very aggressive against Q.6.a. & c. but soon ceased upon our retaliating on suspected Hd-Qrs etc in MARCOING.	

D. D. & L., London, E.C. (A5001) Wt. W1771/M2031 750,000 5/17 Sch. 52 Forms/C2118/14

Army Form C. 2118.

Instructions regarding War Diaries and Intelligence Summaries are contained in F. S. Regs., Part II. and the Staff Manual respectively. Title pages will be prepared in manuscript.

WAR DIARY
or
INTELLIGENCE SUMMARY.

(Erase heading not required.)

Place	Date	Hour	Summary of Events and Information	Remarks and references to Appendices
K 36 a 6 0	February 12th		Movement was seen and engaged in L 23 d. during the morning. This caused a large explosion (probably an ammunition dump set on fire) Hostile Artillery Nil. Night firing tasks carried out.	Sheet 57 C I/10.000.
	13th		Registrations checked by all Batteries in anticipation of relief . Night firing tasks carried out.	
	14th		Quiet day. During the afternoon one Section~~s~~ of each Battery were relieved by corresponding section from 317th Brigade R.F.A., 63rd Division, and on relief moved to their wagon lines.	
	15th		Remainder of relief completed and command of Left Artillery Group handed over to C.C. 317 Bde: R.F.A. at 12 noon.	
	16th to 28th		Ordinary Brigade Routine carried out including general cleaning up, repairing of line gear, refitting of equipment and short tactical exercises. On 27th inst the Brigade took part in a Divisional Artillery exercise carried out in the vicinity of VELU.	

[illegible signature]

Captain R.F.A.

Adjutant 88th Brigade R.F.A.

for Lt Col Cmdg 88th Bde

D. D. & L., London, E.C. (A8001) Wt. W1771/M2031 750,000 5/17 Sch. 52 Forms/C2118/14

19th Divisional Artillery

WAR
DIARY

88th ~~INFANTRY~~ BRIGADE R.F.A.

MARCH 1 9 1 8

WAR DIARY
or
INTELLIGENCE SUMMARY.
(Erase heading not required.)

Instructions regarding War Diaries and Intelligence Summaries are contained in F. S. Regs., Part II. and the Staff Manual respectively. Title pages will be prepared in manuscript.

Army Form C. 2118.

88 Bde R.F.A.

Vol 32

Place	Date	Hour	Summary of Events and Information	Remarks and references to Appendices
YTRES	1.3.18		88th Brigade R.F.A. in rest at YTRES. Ordinary daily routine, cleaning up and preparation for action. Tactical exercise carried out in the vicinity of LE TRANSLOY in cooperation with Aeroplane and 57 INF BDE.	57c 1/40.000
	2.3.18		Ordinary daily routine, cleaning up and preparation for action.	
	3.3.18		Reconnoitring parties visited batteries and H.Q. of 236 BDE R.F.A. preparatory to taking over. One section of each battery relieved corresponding section 236 BDE in the evening.	
	4.3.18		Relief of 236 F.A.B. completed. 88th F.A.B. now covering 63rd DIV. in the FLESQUIERES Sector and under the orders of 63 D.A. H.Q. 88th F.A.B. at Q 3 d 14. Batteries in the area K 26 K 27 K 33 K 34	
Q 3 d 14	5.3.18		Rearrangements of battery positions projected. Harassing fire carried out throughout day and night.	
	6.3.18 / 7.3.18		Rearrangement of battery position carried out. Location of batteries A/88 K 34 a 81 B/88 K 34 a 34 C/88 K 26 b 24 D K 33 b 74. A/88 B/88 D/88 with advanced sections. All firing carried out by advanced sections, main positions being silent except in the case of S.O.S.	
	8.3.18		Daily programme of harassing fire carried out.	
	9.3.18		Harassing fire carried out throughout the day. At 7 p.m. programme in support of a raid by 188 INF. BDE. was carried out until 7.30.	

A6945 Wt. W11422/M1160 350,000 12/16 D. D. & L. Forms/C./2118/14.

Army Form C. 2118.

Instructions regarding War Diaries and Intelligence Summaries are contained in F. S. Regs., Part II. and the Staff Manual respectively. Title pages will be prepared in manuscript.

WAR DIARY
or
INTELLIGENCE SUMMARY.
(Erase heading not required.)

Place	Date	Hour	Summary of Events and Information	Remarks and references to Appendices
Q 3 d. 14	10.3.18		During the morning movement at L1c and E25 was observed and engaged. HAVRINCOURT WOOD was intermittently shelled throughout the morning	
	11.3.18		Daily programme of harassing fire carried out. Very heavy gas shell bombardment of TRESCAULT and GRAND RAVINE from 11.30 till dawn	
	12.3.18		Hostile gas shell bombardment of TRESCAULT and GRAND RAVINE commencing at 8.30 AM and lasting until 12.0 NOON.	
	13.3.18		Hostile fire increased. GRAND RAVINE, FLESQUIERES and HAVRINCOURT shelled throughout the night with guns of all calibres. Harassing fire carried out by batteries according to programme	
	14.3.18		Usual programme of harassing fire carried out. Hostile artillery active throughout the night.	
	15.3.18		" " " " " " " " " " " "	
	16.3.18		" " " " " " " " " " " "	
	17.3.18		" " " " " " " " " " " "	
	18.3.18		" " " " " " " " " " " "	
			Operated in conjunction with a raid by 188th INF BDE.	

A6945 Wt. W11422/M1160 350,000 12/16 D. D. & L. Forms/C./2118/14.

Instructions regarding War Diaries and Intelligence Summaries are contained in F. S. Regs., Part II. and the Staff Manual respectively. Title pages will be prepared in manuscript.

WAR DIARY
or
INTELLIGENCE SUMMARY.
(Erase heading not required.)

Army Form C. 2118.

Place	Date	Hour	Summary of Events and Information	Remarks and references to Appendices
Q3 d 14	19.3.18		Daily programme of harassing fire carried on throughout the day and night. Movement in Square F26 seen and engaged.	
	20.3.18		Daily programme carried out, intermittent shelling of forward areas throughout the night	
	21.3.18	4.45AM	The Enemy attacked accompanied by a bombardment of great violence. All our battery positions received attention with guns of all calibres and gas shell.	
		12 Noon	Bombardment still in progress.	
		4.30pm	Enemy reported holding DOIGNIES. Batteries withdrawn to intermediate positions under cover of darkness. Locations A/88 P2d B/88 P2a C/88 P2a D/88 P2d. H.Q remained at Q3 d 14	
NEUVILLE BOURJONVAL	22.3.18		Enemy attacked again. Retired to positions covering the second system in P6 under cover of darkness. H.Q to NEUVILLE.	
	23.3.18	1.0pm	Withdrew to positions covering the Green line near BARASTRE. Location of Bde O32a	
	24.3.18	9.0am.	Enemy occupy BUS. Withdrew to positions near LE TRANSLOY leaving sections of B/88 C/88 D/88 to cover withdrawal. The whole Brigade complete in action in N23 b2d. by 10.0 A.M.	

A6945 Wt. W11422/M1160 350,000 12/16 D. D. & L. Forms/C./2118/14.

Instructions regarding War Diaries and Intelligence Summaries are contained in F. S. Regs., Part II. and the Staff Manual respectively. Title pages will be prepared in manuscript.

WAR DIARY
or
INTELLIGENCE SUMMARY.
(*Erase heading not required.*)

Army Form C. 2118.

Place	Date	Hour	Summary of Events and Information	Remarks and references to Appendices
	24.3.18	2.30 pm	Enemy reported at MORVAL and were seen moving West along MORVAL RIDGES. Received orders to bring the Brigade into action against enemy about MORVAL but before this order could be carried out H.Q. 63RD D.A. ordered withdrawal to BAZENTIN VIA BEAULENCOURT.	
		3.15 pm	Brigade moved through BEAULENCOURT by the LE SARS road. Owing to congestion of traffic there were frequent halts of from five minutes to half an hour under fire and it was not until 4.45 pm that the head of 88th Brigade R.F.A. Column arrived at the cross-roads at [illegible] A serious block occurred here and H.Q. 63RD D.A. ordered the Brigade to march by FLERS.	
		5.15 pm	88th Brigade passed through FLERS and moved West by a track. There had not been time for a complete reconnaissance and after half a mile of bad going the track ceased and the rest of the march was over shell hole area full of trenches and wire and progress became very slow. At dusk the head of the column had arrived SOUTH of HIGH WOOD and had about half a mile to go to reach the railway but the column was much scattered with 3 guns in a hopeless position about 1000 YDS in rear of the main column. Orders were then given to destroy and abandon these three guns. Almost immediately afterwards an enemy patrol about 30 strong evaded the Brigade defences in the Southern flank and attacked the 3 guns.	

A6945 Wt. W11422/M1160 350,000 12/16 D. D. & L. Forms/C./2118/14.

Instructions regarding War Diaries and Intelligence Summaries are contained in F. S. Regs., Part II. and the Staff Manual respectively. Title pages will be prepared in manuscript.

WAR DIARY
or
INTELLIGENCE SUMMARY.
(Erase heading not required.)

Army Form C. 2118.

Place	Date	Hour	Summary of Events and Information	Remarks and references to Appendices
	24.3.18	10.0 pm	After visiting the rendezvous BYSANTIN LE PETIT, which was evacuated, proceeded to vicinity of HENENCOURT and formed a wagon line with details of Brigade.	
	25.3.18		H.Q and A/88 to VADENCOURT, B/88 and D/88 to WARLOY	
		10.0 pm	C/88 arrived at WARLOY	
HERISSART	26.3.18		Brigade marched to HERISSART to refit under orders from V Corps	
	27.3.18		Brigade marched to MARIEUX	
	28.3.18		Brigade marched to BERTEAUCOURT under orders from III Army	
BERTEAUCOURT	29.3.18		BERTEAUCOURT.	
	30.3.18		— ditto —	
	31.3.18		To BOURBERS SUR CANCHE preparatory to entraining for the north	

[signature] Capt
for Lieut Colonel R.F.A.
Commanding 88th Brigade R.F.A

19th Divisional Artillery.

88th BRIGADE R. F. A. ::: APRIL 1918.

19

88 Bde R.F.A. Army Form C. 2118.

Vol 33

WAR DIARY
or
INTELLIGENCE SUMMARY.
(Erase heading not required.)

Instructions regarding War Diaries and Intelligence Summaries are contained in F. S. Regs., Part II. and the Staff Manual respectively. Title pages will be prepared in manuscript.

Place	Date	Hour	Summary of Events and Information	Remarks and references to Appendices
BOUBERS-SUR-CANCHE	1.4.18		Ordinary Brigade routine carried out during the day, during the afternoon and evening Brigade left to entrain at PETIT-HOUVIN and FREVENT for GODEWAERSVELDE	LENS 11 1/100,000
	2.4.18		Brigade arrived at GODEWAERSVELDE and CHESTRE to Wagon lines in the vicinity of BAILLEUL West	
	3.4.18		Batteries ordered into action to positions in vicinity of KEMMEL under the command of O.C 87th Brigade R.F.A. BRIGADE H.Q and Wagon lines moved to Wagon lines in vicinity of S.12 BDE H.Q being established at (S.12.c.54)	SHEET 28 1/40,000
	5.4.18		Brigade H.Q took over command of 25th D.A. pending arrival of 25th D.A. H.Q. The H.Q were established at (S.17.c.58)	
ROUBLSBERG CAMP S.17.c.58	6.4.18 to 9.4.18		Duties of 25th DIV C.R.A carried out — Batteries of 88th F.A. Brigade still remaining under orders of O.C. F.A. Brigade	
	10.4.18		25th D.A. H.Q arrived and assumed command of their D.A. and Bde H.Q returned to their Wagon lines at (S.17.a.54)	
	11.4.18		Brigade H.Q and Battery Wagon lines moved to new Wagon lines between BRULOOZE and LOCRE	
	12.4.18		Ordinary daily routine carried out	

A6945 Wt. W11422/M1160 350,000 12/16 D. D. & L. Forms/C.2118/14.

Instructions regarding War Diaries and Intelligence Summaries are contained in F. S. Regs., Part II. and the Staff Manual respectively. Title pages will be prepared in manuscript.

WAR DIARY
or
INTELLIGENCE SUMMARY.
(*Erase heading not required.*)

Army Form C. 2118.

Place	Date	Hour	Summary of Events and Information	Remarks and references to Appendices
LOCRE	13.4.18		Brigade H.Q and Battery Wagon lines moved to new Wagon lines just outside WESTOUTRE. Arriving there by ~~noon~~ 12. NOON.	SHEET 28 1/40,000
	14.4.18 to 16.4.18		Ordinary daily routine carried out " " " " "	
	17.4.18		Brigade H.Q moved to new Wagon line at (G 33 b 66) and Battery Wagon lines moved to vicinity of G 28 + 29	
	18.4.18 to 24.4.18		Ordinary daily routine carried out " " " " " At about 7.0 pm on 24th very heavy bombardment started and continued throughout the night and most part of the 25th	
	25.4.18		At 3.30 a.m H.Q moved to Wagon line at L.21.A.3.6 Brigade H.Q ordered to form LAISON between 19th Div Artillery and 28th French Div Artillery (MERCERS GROUP) H.Q being established at HOOGRAF CABARET	SHEET 27 1/40,000
	26.4.18		LAISON duties carried out – Batteries ~~88~~ 88th Brigade still remaining under orders of O.C 87 F A BDE. Wagon lines 88th Bde to vicinity of L 21 + L 14.	
	27.4.18		All Batteries and H.Q withdrawn from action to their Wagon lines	

A6945 Wt. W11422/M1160 350,000 12/16 D. D. & L. Forms/C.2118/14.

Army Form C. 2118.

WAR DIARY
or
INTELLIGENCE SUMMARY.
(Erase heading not required.)

Instructions regarding War Diaries and Intelligence Summaries are contained in F. S. Regs., Part II. and the Staff Manual respectively. Title pages will be prepared in manuscript.

Place	Date	Hour	Summary of Events and Information	Remarks and references to Appendices
L21 c	28.4.18		Ordinary Brigade routine, cleaning up and generally refitting commenced	Ref Sheet 27
	29.4.18		The Brigade marched from Wagon lines VIA STEENVORDE - BABINCOVE - EBBLINGHEM - BELLE CROIX to billets in the vicinity of CAMPAGNE	
	30.4.18		Ordinary Brigade routine refitting and cleaning continued	

[illegible signature] Capt

for Lieut Colonel R.F.A

Commanding 88th Brigade R.F.A

A6945 Wt. W11422/M1160 350,000 12/16 D. D. & L. Forms/C./2118/14.

Instructions regarding War Diaries and Intelligence Summaries are contained in F. S. Regs., Part II. and the Staff Manual respectively. Title pages will be prepared in manuscript.

WAR DIARY
or
INTELLIGENCE SUMMARY.
(*Erase heading not required.*)

88 Bde R.F.A.
19
May. Vol 34

Army Form C. 2118.

Place	Date	Hour	Summary of Events and Information	Remarks and references to Appendices
CHAMPAGNE	1st to 17th		The Brigade were in XVII Corps Reserve in billets about CHAMPAGNE. During this period ordinary Brigade Routine was carried out, cleaning up & re-equipping. In addition two inspections were made on 1st & 3rd inst. by the G.O.C. R.A. 2nd Army, & G.O.C., R.A. XVII Corps respectively	Sheet 27 & 28 1/40,000
	18th		Early in the morning the Brigade commenced entraining at WIZERNES & proceeded via ETAPLES - NOYELLES-sur-MER - St DENNIS - CHATEAU THIERRY - EPERNAY to CHALONS where they detrained on the 19th inst and proceeded to camp at DAMPIERRE-sur-MOIVRE.	
DAMPIERRE-sur-MOIVRE	20th to 27th		Ordinary Brigade Routine carried out	French Map Sheet CHALONS 1/200,000
	28th		The Brigade moved via LONGEVAS - St MEMMIE - CHALONS - JUVIGNY - TOURS-sur-MARNE to BISSEUIL where billets were taken for the night	
BISSEUIL	29th		March resumed via AY - CUMIERES - HAUTVILLERS - NANTEUIL - MARFAUX - to CHAMUZY where wagon lines were established. During the afternoon the Brigade moved into action just N of SARCY; H.Q. being established in the village	
SARCY	30		Quiet night. In the early morning the enemy attacked & our own Infantry took. Batteries were withdrawn to positions near Xroads between CHAMUZY & SARCY. In the evening Batteries were again withdrawn to positions about CHAMUZY village. Bde H.Q. being established in the village.	SOISSONS

D. D. & L., London, E.C. (A8001) Wt. W2771/M2031 750,000 5/17 Sch. 52 Forms/C2118/14

Instructions regarding War Diaries and Intelligence Summaries are contained in F. S. Regs., Part II. and the Staff Manual respectively. Title pages will be prepared in manuscript.

WAR DIARY
or
INTELLIGENCE SUMMARY.
(Erase heading not required.)

Army Form C. 2118.

Place	Date	Hour	Summary of Events and Information	Remarks and references to Appendices
CHAHOZY	31st		Quiet throughout the night. During the day all roads & tracks & likely places of assembly within group zone were kept under bursts of fire.	SOISSONS

[illegible] Lieut Col. RFA
Commanding 88 Brigade RFA

D. D. & L., London, E.C.
(A8001) Wt. W1771/M2031 750,000 5/17 Sch. 52 Forms/C2118/14

Instructions regarding War Diaries and Intelligence Summaries are contained in F. S. Regs., Par. II. and the Staff Manual respectively. Title pages will be prepared in manuscript.

WAR DIARY
or
INTELLIGENCE SUMMARY.
(Erase heading not required.)

Army Form C. 2118.

88 Bde R F A
Vol 35

Place	Date	Hour	Summary of Events and Information	Remarks and references to Appendices
CHAMUZY	1st June		The Brigade were in action about CHAMUZY and Bde: H.Q. established in CHAMUZY Village. In addition 2 Batteries of French 75 mm were attached and the whole known as TOVEY's GROUP, and covered the front held by the 56th Infantry Brigade. During the afternoon owing to a local attack by the enemy Batteries were withdrawn to positions between NAPPES & CHAMUZY and Bde: Hd-Qrs to BULLEN WOOD.	JONCHERY I/20.000
BULLEN	2nd		From 3.0am onwards, roads, tracks and likely places of assembly within enemy lines were searched by our fire. Except for occasional shelling of CHAMUZY & BLIGNY hostile artillery was very quiet.	
	3rd		Situation unchanged. In the afternoon movement was observed about VILLE en TARDENOIS and engaged. Harrassing fire carried out throughout the night on roads and likely places of assembly.	
	4th		Situation unchanged. Movement, suspected strong points and other suitable objectives were engaged throughout the day. In view of a possible attack by the enemy on our front, counter-preparation was carried out inthe evening and again at 2.0am and 3.0am (5th).	
	5th		Quiet day. Usual firing carried out. Hostile Arty: fairly active against Battery positions about 94.93, BOIS d' ECLISSES, and BOIS d'AULNAY, in the evening.	
	6th		At about 5.0am the enemy attacked and captured MONTAGNE DE BLIGNY, but this was retaken by	

A6945 Wt. W11422/M1160 350,000 12/16 D. D. & L. Forms/C./2118/14.

Instructions regarding War Diaries and Intelligence Summaries are contained in F. S. Regs., Part II, and the Staff Manual respectively. Title pages will be prepared in manuscript.

WAR DIARY
or
INTELLIGENCE SUMMARY.
(*Erase heading not required.*)

Army Form C. 2118.

Place	Date	Hour	Summary of Events and Information	Remarks and references to Appendices
BULLEN	6th	(contd)	our troops later in the day by a counter attack, together with about 200 prisoners.	JONCHERY I/20.000
			In the evening Bde: H.Q. were withdrawn to position in wood about. BOIS de COUTRON	
	7th) 8th)		Situation unchanged. Usual firing carried out each day. Hostile Arty: on the whole was quiet except for occasional bursts of fire on BLIGNY and BOIS d' ECLISSES.	
	9th		At about 3.10am the enemy put down a very heavy barrage of gas & H.E. on our front and "Counter preparation" by our Batteries commenced. No hostile attack however developed.	
			Considerable movement was seen in SARCY in the afternoon and engaged.	
	10th		During the day our Arty: engaged movement & carried out registrations on selected points.	
			By night special targets were subjected to harrassing fire.	
	11th to) 15th)		Situation still unchanged. programme of the 10th inst repeated each day.	
	16th		On the night 2 guns of each of the 8th, 9th & 10th Italian Batteries came into action at positions of A/88, B/88, and D/88 respectively, and arrangements made to hand over to these Batteries.	
	17th		Remaining 2 guns of each of the Italian Batteries came into action & registered and the guns of the 88th Brigade were withdrawn to positions in the close vicinity.	

A6945 Wt. W11422/M1160 350,000 12/16 D. D. & L. Forms/C./2118/14.

Instructions regarding War Diaries and Intelligence Summaries are contained in F. S. Regs., Par. II, and the Staff Manual respectively. Title pages will be prepared in manuscript.

WAR DIARY
or
INTELLIGENCE SUMMARY.
(Erase heading not required.)

Army Form C. 2118.

Place	Date	Hour	Summary of Events and Information	Remarks and references to Appendices
[illegible]	18th		During the day final arrangements for the relief were made and in the evening Batteries withdrew their guns etc to the wagon lines near HAUTVILLERS.	SOISSONS I/100.000
	20th		The Brigade marched via EPERNAY and CHOUILLY to VERTUS where billets were taken for the night.	CHALONS I/80.000.,
	21st		March resumed via BERGERES and COLLIGNY to BANNES.	ARCIS I/80.000.
BANNES	22nd to) 29th)		Ordinary Brigade Routine carried out including cleaning up, overhaul of equipment guns etc.	
	30th		The Brigade marched via FERE CHAMPENOISE - CONNANTRAY - SOMMESOUS to MAILLY le CAMP where they entrained for HESDIN.	
			[signature] Lieut: Col: R.F.A. Commanding 88th Brigade R. F. A.	

A6945 Wt. W11422/M1160 350,000 12/16 D. D. & L. Forms/C./2118/14.

CORPS D'ARMEE — Q.G. le 1[illegible] Juin 1918

ARTILLERIE

Etat-Major

O R D R E N° . 84

Le Colonel [illegible] Commandant l'Artillerie du 9e Corps d'Armée cite à l'ORDRE DE LA BRIGADE :

Lieutenant (f.fons. de Major) Thomas James [illegible]
(Bie. "C" de la 87 Brigade R.F.A., 1re Division)

"A donné un bel exemple de bravoure le 30 Mai 1918, au moment où l'infanterie se repliait, en maintenant sa batterie en action sous un fort bombardement, tirant à vue sur l'ennemi sans arrêt et encourageant ses hommes par son exemple et son mépris du danger jusqu'au moment où il fut blessé".

Lieutenant Edward Alfred [illegible]
(Batterie "D" de la 88e Brigade R.F.A. 19e Division)

"Etant en liaison avec l'Infanterie les 4 et 5 Juin 1918 a montré une grande bravoure en réglant le feu de sa batterie d'observatoires avancés très exposés, sous un sévère bombardement. Son téléphone et son poste optique ayant été détruits par le feu ennemi, a continué à observer et rétabli les communications".

L/Bombardier John [illegible]
(Mle. [illegible] - Batterie "A" de la 88e Brigade RFA)

"Belle conduite du 29 Mai au 6 Juin 1918. Le 6 Juin, alors que tous les hommes de son peloton de pièce étaient tués ou blessés, à l'exception de lui-même et d'un autre, a maintenu sa pièce en action pendant toute la durée de la contre préparation; est allé ensuite en reconnaissance à travers un tir de barrage et a rapporté des renseignements utiles sur la situation".

Sergent Gordon Edward H U G H E S
(Mle. [illegible], Batterie "C" de la 87e Brigade R.F.A.)

"Le 30 Mai 1918 et bien qu'il fut blessé, a continué à commander sa pièce sous un fort bombardement. Pendant que sa batterie se repliait par ordre a refusé d'aller au poste de secours jusqu'à ce que la nouvelle position ait été occupée et que son peloton de pièce ait été en sûreté hors de la zone bombardée".

Canonnier John [illegible]
(Mle. 109406 - Batterie "D" de la 87e Brigade R.F.A.)

"A fait preuve de bravoure et de dévouement dans l'accomplissement de son devoir, le 6 Juin 1918, en allant continuellement et sous un fort bombardement réparer la ligne téléphonique entre sa batterie et le poste d'observation. Ce fut en grande partie grâce à son courage et à son énergie que la ligne fut maintenue toute la journée, permettant ainsi à la batterie de prendre à partie et de briser des formations ennemies à plusieurs reprises".

L/Bombardier....

L/Bombardier Peter [illegible]
(Mle. [illegible] - batterie "[illegible]" de la [illegible] Brigade R.F.A.)

"Entre le 29 Mai et le 6 Juin 1918 a montré une bravoure et un sang-froid constants en assurant la liaison optique et les reconnaissances. Le 6 Juin, la fumée empêchant le fonctionnement des signaux optiques, a avancé une ligne téléphonique jusqu'à une position très exposée et l'a maintenue sous un fort bombardement".

Sergent Maréchal-Ferrant Edward - Leslie [illegible]
Mle. [illegible] - 1re Colonne de Munitions).

"A fait preuve de bravoure et de dévouement dans l'accomplissement de son devoir dans la nuit du [illegible] Mai au [illegible] Juin, comme chef d'un convoi de [illegible] voitures qui portait des munitions aux positions de batteries : les approches étant fortement bombardées ce sous-officier sachant que l'on avait un besoin urgent de munitions, poussa en avant et par sa détermination et son exemple réussit à ravitailler les pièces".

Conducteur John Ernest [illegible]
(Mle. [illegible] Colonne de Munitions de la [illegible],
section n° [illegible]

"A rendu constamment les meilleurs services et fait preuve d'un grand dévouement du 28 Mai au 10 Juin 1918; dans un ravitaillement des positions de batteries, sa voiture ayant été séparée du convoi par suite d'un violent bombardement de la route, ce conducteur en prit la direction et réussit à trouver la batterie et à délivrer les munitions en bonnes mains".

Sergent Rufus Rodgers [illegible]
Mle. 45947 - Batterie "[illegible]" de la [illegible] Brigade R.F.A.)

"Le 6 Juin 1918, comme plus ancien sous-officier de l'échelon avancé, a fait preuve de grand sang-froid et d'initiative en repliant et les hommes et les chevaux sous un fort bombardement; est resté sur place jusqu'à ce que tout fût enlevé montrant à tous un exemple digne d'éloges".

Sergent-Major de Batterie Edward [illegible]
(Mle. [illegible] - Batterie "[illegible]" de la [illegible] Brigade R.F.A.)

"A rendu de grands services du 30 Mai au 10 Juin 1918 période pendant laquelle il eut seul la charge des échelons pendant l'absence de tous les Officiers et assura par son énergie infatigable un approvisionnement suffisant de munitions aux positions de batteries. Il eut fréquemment à conduire ses caissons sous de forts bombardements et montra un complet mépris du danger".

Le Colonel [illegible] Cdt. l'Art. du [illegible]

[signature]

[illegible] D'ARMÉE
[illegible]
[illegible]

Q.G. le 14 Juin 1918

O R D R E N° 64

Le Colonel H A R D Y Commandant l'Artillerie du 9e Corps d'Armée cite à l'ORDRE DE LA BRIGADE :

Lieutenant (f.fons. de Major) Thomas James [illegible]
(Bie. "C" de la 87 Brigade R.F.A., 19e Division)

"A donné un bel exemple de bravoure le 30 Mai 1918, au moment où l'infanterie se repliait, en maintenant sa batterie en action sous un fort bombardement, tirant à vue sur l'ennemi sans arrêt et encourageant ses hommes par son exemple et son mépris du danger jusqu'au moment où il fut blessé".

Lieutenant Edward Alfred B I S H O P
(Batterie "D" de la 88e Brigade R.F.A. 19e Division)

"Étant en liaison avec l'Infanterie les 4 et 5 Juin 1918 a montré une réelle bravoure en réglant le feu de sa batterie d'observatoires très exposés, sous un sévère bombardement. Son téléphone et son poste optique ayant été détruits par le feu ennemi, a continué à observer et rétabli les communications".

[illegible] John L A N G T O N
([illegible] - Batterie "[illegible]" de la 88e Brigade RFA)

"Belle conduite du 29 Mai au 6 Juin 1918. Le 6 Juin, alors que tous les hommes de son peloton de pièce étaient tués ou blessés, à l'exception de lui-même et d'un autre, a maintenu sa pièce en action pendant toute la durée de la contre-préparation; est allé ensuite en reconnaissance à travers un tir de barrage et a rapporté des renseignements utiles sur la situation".

Sergent Gordon Edward H U G H E S
(Mle. [illegible], Batterie "C" de la 87e Brigade R.F.A.)

"Le 28 Mai 1918, et bien qu'il fût blessé, a continué à commander sa pièce sous un fort bombardement. Pendant que sa batterie se repliait par échelons, a refusé d'aller au poste de secours jusqu'à ce que la nouvelle position ait été occupée et que son peloton de pièce ait été en sûreté hors de la zone [illegible]".

Canonnier John [illegible]
(Mle. [illegible] - Batterie [illegible] de la [illegible] Brigade R.F.A.)

"A fait preuve de bravoure et de dévouement [illegible] de son devoir, le [illegible] Juin 1918, en [illegible] sous un fort bombardement [illegible] la ligne [illegible] batterie et le poste d'observation [illegible]

L/Bombardier Peter B E R R Y
(Mle. 18452 - batterie "B" de la 88° Brigade R.F.A.).

"Entre le 29 Mai et le 6 Juin 1918 a montré une bravoure et un sang-froid constants en assurant la liaison optique et les reconnaissances. Le 6 Juin la fumée empêchant le fonctionnement des signaux optiques a avancé une ligne téléphonique jusqu'à une position très exposée et l'a maintenu sous un fort bombardement".

Sergent Maréchal-ferrant Edward - Leslie B E D D I E
Mle. 41368 - 19° Colonne de Munitions).

"A fait preuve de bravoure et de dévouement dans l'accomplissement de son devoir dans la nuit du 31 Mai au 1° Juin, comme chef d'un convoi de 6 voitures qui portait des munitions aux positions de batteries : les approches étant fortement bombardées ce sous-officier sachant que l'ont avait un besoin urgent de munitions, poussa en avant et par sa détermination et son exemple réussit à ravitailler les pièces".

Conducteur John Ernest H O D S O N
(Mle. 99307 Colonne de Munitions de la 19° D.I. section n° 1)

"A rendu constamment les meilleurs services a fait preuve d'un grand dévouement du 29 Mai au 10 Juin 1918; Dans un ravitaillement des positions de batteries, sa voiture ayant été séparée du convoi par suite d'un violent bombardement de la route, ce conducteur en prit la direction et réussit à trouver la batterie et à délivrer les munitions en bonnes mains".

Sergent Rufus Rodgers B A I R D
Mle. 45947 - Batterie "D" de la 88° Brigade R.F.A.)

"Le 6 Juin 1918, comme plus ancien sous-Officier de l'échelon avancé a fait preuve de grand sang-froid et d'initiative en repliant et les hommes et les chevaux sous un fort bombardement, est resté sur place jusqu'à ce que tout fut enlevé montrant à tous un exemple digne d'éloges".

Sergent-Major de Batterie Edward G A R T O N
(Mle. 31121 - Batterie "B" de la 87° Brigade R.F.A.)

"A rendu de grands services du 30 Mai au 10 Juin 1918 période pendant laquelle il eut seul la charge des échelons pendant l'absence de tous les Officiers et assura par son énergie infatigable un approvisionnement suffisant de munitions aux positions de batteries. Il eut fréquemment à conduire ses caissons sous de forts bombardements et montra un complet mépris du danger".

Le Colonel TARDY Cdt. l'Art. du 9° C.A.

[illegible] Corps d'Armée
ARTILLERIE
Etat-Major

Q.G. le 11 Juin 1918

ORDRE N° [illegible]

Le Colonel [illegible] Commandant l'Artillerie du 5e Corps d'Armée cite à l'ORDRE DE LA DIVISION :

Lieutenant (f.fons. de Major) Thomas James [illegible]
(Btie. "D" de la 87e Brigade R.F.A., 19e Division)

"A donné un bel exemple de bravoure le 27 mai 1918, au moment où l'infanterie se repliait, en maintenant sa batterie en action sous un fort bombardement, tirant à vue sur l'ennemi pour arrêter [illegible] et encourageant ses hommes par son exemple et son mépris du danger jusqu'au moment où il fut blessé".

Lieutenant Edmund Alfred [illegible]
(Batterie "D" de la 87e Brigade R.F.A. 19e Division)

"Etant en liaison avec l'infanterie les 6 et 7 Juin 1918 a montré une réelle bravoure en réglant le tir de sa batterie d'observatoires très exposés, sous un sévère bombardement. Son téléphone et son poste optique ayant été détruits par le feu ennemi, a continué d'observer et rétabli les communications".

L/Bombardier John [illegible]
(Mle. [illegible] - Batterie "D" de la 87e Brigade RFA)

"Belle conduite du 27 Mai au 6 Juin 1918. Le 6 Juin, alors que tous les hommes de son peloton de pièce étaient tués ou blessés, à l'exception de lui-même et d'un autre, a maintenu sa pièce en action pendant toute la durée de la contre préparation; est allé ensuite en reconnaissance à travers un tir de barrage et a rapporté des renseignements utiles sur la situation".

Sergent Gordon Edmund HUGHES
(Mle. [illegible], Batterie "D" de la 87e Brigade R.F.A.)

"Le 28 Mai 1918, bien qu'il fût blessé, a continué à commander sa pièce sous un fort bombardement. Pendant que sa batterie se repliait sur ordre, a refusé d'aller au poste de secours jusqu'à ce que la nouvelle position ait été occupée et que son peloton de pièce ait été en sûreté hors de la zone bombardée".

Gunner John DUNSTAN
(Mle. [illegible] - Batterie "D" de la 87e Brigade R.F.A.)

"A fait preuve de bravoure et de dévouement dans l'accomplissement de son devoir le 6 Juin 1918, en allant continuellement et sous un fort bombardement réparer la ligne téléphonique entre sa batterie et le poste d'observation. Ce fut en grande partie grâce à son courage et à son énergie que la ligne fut maintenue toute la journée, permettant ainsi à la batterie de prendre à partie et de briser des formations ennemies à plusieurs reprises".

L/Bombardier.../...

562

L/Bombardier Peter [illegible]
(Mle. [illegible] - Batterie "[illegible]" de la [illegible])

"Entre le 29 Mai et le 6 Juin 1918 a montré une bravoure et un sang-froid constants en assurant les liaisons optiques et les reconnaissances. Le 6 Juin, [illegible] le fonctionnement des signaux optiques, a [illegible] une ligne [illegible] jusqu'à une position très exposée et l'a maintenue sous un fort bombardement".

Sergent Maréchal-Ferrant [illegible] - Leslie [illegible]
(Mle. [illegible] - [illegible] Colonne de Munitions).

"A fait preuve de bravoure et de dévouement dans l'accomplissement de son devoir dans la nuit du [illegible] Mai au [illegible] Juin, comme chef d'un convoi de [illegible] voitures qui portait des munitions aux positions de batteries ; les approches étant fortement [illegible] ce sous-officier [illegible] que l'on avait un besoin [illegible] de munitions, [illegible] et par sa détermination et son [illegible] réussit à [illegible]".

Conducteur John Ernest [illegible]
(Mle. [illegible] - Colonne de Munitions de la [illegible]
Section n° 1)

"A rendu constamment les meilleurs services et fait preuve d'un grand dévouement du 29 Mai au 10 Juin 1918 ; dans un convoi allant des positions de batteries, sa voiture ayant été séparée du convoi par suite d'un violent bombardement de la route, ce conducteur en prit la direction et réussit à trouver [illegible] et à délivrer les munitions en bonnes [illegible]".

Sergent Rufus Rodney [illegible]
(Mle. [illegible] - Batterie "[illegible]" de la [illegible])

"Le 6 Juin 1918, comme plus ancien sous-officier de l'[illegible] a fait preuve de grand sang-froid et d'initiative en [illegible] et les hommes et les chevaux sous un fort bombardement ; est resté sur place jusqu'à ce que tout fût [illegible] donnant à tous un exemple digne d'éloges".

Sergent-Major de Batterie Edward [illegible]
(Mle. [illegible] - Batterie "[illegible]" de la [illegible])

"A rendu de grands services du [illegible] Mai au 10 Juin 1918 période pendant laquelle il eut seul la charge [illegible] des échelons pendant l'absence de tous les Officiers et assura par son énergie infatigable un approvisionnement suffisant de munitions aux positions de batteries. Il eut fréquemment à conduire [illegible] caissons sous de forts bombardements et montra un complet mépris du danger".

Le Colonel [illegible] Cdt. l'Art. de [illegible]

[illegible]

Army Form C. 2118.

88 Bde R F A

Vol 36

Instructions regarding War Diaries and Intelligence Summaries are contained in F. S. Regs., Part II. and the Staff Manual respectively. Title pages will be prepared in manuscript.

WAR DIARY
or
INTELLIGENCE SUMMARY.
(Erase heading not required.)

Place	Date	Hour	Summary of Events and Information	Remarks and references to Appendices
	2nd July		The Brigade arrived at HESDIN and detrained. Marched via FRUGES - FAUQUEMBERGUES to MERCK St. LIEVEN where billets were taken.	LENS II & HAZEBROUCK I/100,000
MERCK-St-LIEVEN	3rd to 12th July		Ordinary Brigade Routine carried out, including Tactical exercises, cleaning up and refitting of equipment and overhaul of guns.	
	13th July		The Brigade marched via FAUQUEMBERGUES - COYECQUE - to BOMY. Hd-Qrs were billetted in BOMY "A" & "B" Batteries in RUPIGNY and "C" & "D" Batteries in GREUPPE.	
	14th to 21st July		Brigade training continued.	
	21st July		Moved via GREUPPE - BEAUMETZ -les-AIRE - LAIRES to FEBVIN PALFART.	
	22nd to 31st July		Brigade training, including calibration of guns, firing practice on WESTREHEM ARTY: RANGE and Signalling Schemes.	
			[signature] Major R.F.A. Commanding 88th Brigade R. F. A	

A6945 Wt. W11422/M1160 350,000 12/16 D. D. & L. Forms/C./2118/14.

LEFT ARTILLERY GROUP, 19TH DIVISION.

Instructions regarding War Diaries and Intelligence Summaries are contained in F. S. Regs., Part II. and the Staff Manual respectively. Title pages will be prepared in manuscript.

WAR DIARY
or
INTELLIGENCE SUMMARY.

(*Erase heading not required.*)

Army Form C. 2118.

Place	Date	Hour	Summary of Events and Information	Remarks and references to Appendices
HERVIN . PALFART.	AUG. 1st		Brigade training, including musketry, physical training, gun-drill etc.	
	2nd		Brigade Signalling Scheme. Usual training programme carried out.	
	3rd		Preparations for moving into action	
	4/5th.		" " " " "	
Sheet 36a SE 1/40,000. BOIS DES DAME.	6th.		Brigade moved into temporary wagon lines in BOIS DES DAMES. One section per Battery relieves corresponding Batteries of 47th Brigade, R.F.A, 3rd Division, after dark as follows:- A/88 relieves 6th Battery, B"/88 relieves 23rd Battery, C/88 relieves 49th Battery, "D"/88 relieve 130th Battery. Headquarters remain in BOIS DES DAME.	36A SE 1/20000
Sheet 36a SE 1/40,000. CHATEAU L'ABBAYE. Q 35 e 3 4	7th		Relief of 47th Brigade, RFA completed. H.Q. 88th Brigade established at CHATEAU L'ABBAYE Q 35 e 3 4. Brigade took over wagon lines 47th Brigade, RFA. N. of LAPUGNOY. Locations of Batteries are as follows: "A"/88. 4 guns V 18 c 75 20, 2 guns W 14 b 05 08, "B"/88. 4 guns W 25 b 22 72 and 2 guns W 20 b 20 38. "C"/88. 4 guns W 14 c 48 20, 2 roving guns. "D"/88. 4 hows: E 3 a 33 60, 2 Hows: W 21 c 70 45.	
	8th		Registration carried on throughout the day. Harassing fire, 300 rounds 18-pdr & 4.5.hows; during the night.	

P.T.O.

A5943 Wt. W11422/M1160 350,000 12/16 D. D. & L. Forms/C/2118/14.

(SHEET NO: 2).

Army Form C. 2118.

Instructions regarding War Diaries and Intelligence Summaries are contained in F. S. Regs., Part II. and the Staff Manual respectively. Title pages will be prepared in manuscript.

WAR DIARY
or
INTELLIGENCE SUMMARY.

(Erase heading not required.)

Place	Date	Hour	Summary of Events and Information	Remarks and references to Appendices
	9th		Enemy commenced to retire on Divisional Front. Concentrations fired on VERTBOIS FARM Q 35 d 2 8 at 7.0.am, 8.15.am, 10.0.am. VERTBOIS FARM captured at 10.30.am.	36ASE 1/20000
	10th.		Forward wagon lines established as follows:- "A"/88. V 23 d 5 3, "B"/88. V 30 b 5 6, "C"/88 V 23 d 5 3, "D"/88. D 6 c 5 7. 4 hows "D"/88 moved to W 15 a 7 3, 2 guns "B"/88 to W 20 d 2 4, 2 guns "B"/88 to W 15 c 0 1 on the night 10/11. Harassing fire carried out throughout the night as usual.	
	11/15.		Usual programme of harassing fire carried on throughout the night.	
	16th		"A"/88 send forward a sniping gun to position W 9 b 8 1 and fired on Road at R 25 c 4 4 and R 25 central. Usual harassing fire carried on throughout the night.	
	17th		Usual programme of harassing fire carried out throughout the night.	
	18th		" " " " " " " " " "	
	19th		B/88 send forward a sniping gun to W 9 b 1 1 (9.0.am) and fire on Road R 27 a 35 40 to R 27 a 9 8. Usual harassing fire maintained.	
	20th		4 guns B/88 move to a position W 20 d 2 4. C/88 send forward a sniping gun to W 10 c 8 8 and fire on road from R 34 a 7 9 to R 28 d 65 50. Harassing fire as usual.	
	21st		Harassing fire as usual throughout the night.	

A6945 Wt. W11422/M1160 350,000 12/16 D. D. & L. Forms/C./2118/14.

(SHEET 3)

Army Form C. 2118.

Instructions regarding War Diaries and Intelligence Summaries are contained in F. S. Regs., Part II. and the Staff Manual respectively. Title pages will be prepared in manuscript.

WAR DIARY
or
INTELLIGENCE SUMMARY.
(Erase heading not required.)

Place	Date	Hour	Summary of Events and Information	Remarks and references to Appendices
	22nd.		C/88 send forward a sniping gun in the neighbourhood of W 4 and fire on track R 21 d 17 to R 21 b 7 1.	36ASE 1/20000
			D/88 send forward 1 4.5.how to position in W 10 d and fire on Road in 27 c. Usual harassing fire carried out during the night.	
BOWERS RETREAT. W 7 a 10 15	23rd		88th Brigade, R. F.A. take over from 32nd F.A.B. 4th Division and 65th Army Brigade, RFA come under their orders. H.Q. 88th Brigade, R.F.A. moved to BOWERS RETREAT.	
	24th		4 guns B/88 and 2 4.5.hows are detached, and are sent forward under O.C. B/88 as OUTPOST BATTERY to cover the advance Battalion of infantry. 1 section to Q 34 b 5 3: 1 section to Q 29 c 1 5; 1 section to Q 28 d 7 6. 2 guns C/88 moved to position W 9 b 15 15. Harassing fire as usual.	
	25th		OUTPOST BATTERY fire as requested by the Infantry.	
	26th		65th Army Brigade, R.F.A. withdraw from action. "A"/47 Battery attached to 88th Brigade, RFA.	
	27th		6 guns "C"/88 moved to V 6 d 4 4 to cover the "line of retention ". Fire carried out by OUTPOST BATTERY by arrangement with Infantry Battalion	
	28th		"A"/88 move to position V 6 a 4 2 to cover "line of retention". Advanced section "A"/47 rejoin Battery at W 17 c 8 2. 2 guns "B"/88 moved to Q 30 a.	

(A9175) Wt W2358/P360 600,000 12/17 D. D. & L. Sch. 52a. Forms/C2118/13.

(SHEET 4).

Army Form C. 2118.

WAR DIARY
or
INTELLIGENCE SUMMARY.
(Erase heading not required.)

Instructions regarding War Diaries and Intelligence Summaries are contained in F. S. Regs., Part II. and the Staff Manual respectively. Title pages will be prepared in manuscript.

Place	Date	Hour	Summary of Events and Information	Remarks and references to Appendices
	29th		Wagon Lines of 88th Brigade RFA move to CENSE LA VALLEE and LA VALLEE V 10, V 16.	
	~~[illegible]~~		"D"/47 come under the tactical control of 88th Brigade, RFA.	
			2 section of "D"/88 move from W 15 a 6 3 to Q 28 d 6 5.	
	30th		"A"/88 move to Q 29 d 8 7 and C/88 to Q 29 d 2 5.	
	31st		Headquarters 88th Brigade, RFA move to W 14 b 2 8 at 3.0.pm.	

2.9.18.

[signature] Capt
for Lieut. Colonel, RFA.
Commanding 88th Brigade, RFA.

(A9175) Wt W2353/P360 600,000 12/17 D. D. & L. Sch. 52a. Forms/C2118/15

14

Instructions regarding War Diaries and Intelligence Summaries are contained in F. S. Regs., Part II. and the Staff Manual respectively. Title pages will be prepared in manuscript.

WAR DIARY
or
INTELLIGENCE SUMMARY.
(Erase heading not required.)

88 Bde R.F.A.

Army Form C. 2118.

Sept 18

Place	Date	Hour	Summary of Events and Information	Remarks and references to Appendices
W 14 b 2 8	1st Sept:		Brigade Hd-Qrs moved to X 2 a 5 8 and Batteries moved forward to positions as follows :- A/88 R 27 d 7 2, B/88 R 27 b 7 5, C/88, R 27 d 3 1, D/88 R 21 c 7 2, A/47 R 27 d 4 6, D/47 R 33 b 7 7. Harrassing fire carried out throughout the night.	Sheet 36 SE I/20.000
X 2 a 5 8	2nd Sept:		Quiet day. Harrassing fire carried out during the night on selected objectives within the zone.	
	3rd Sept:		At 5.30am programme in support of attack by the 58th Infantry Brigade carried out. Operations successful and 160 prisoners, including 5 officers, taken.	
	4th Sept) 5th ")		Quiet days. Usual night firing tasks carried out.	
	6th Sept:		Movement and selected objectives engaged during the day and harrassing fire throughout the night. In the evening the Group were reinforced by B/47 and C/47 Batteries. Bde: H.Q. moved to M 31 c 6 7.	
	7th Sept:) 9th Sept:)		Batteries commenced cutting wire within group zone preparatory for an operation to be carried out by the 57th Infantry Brigade. Usual night firing tasks carried out.	
	10th Sept:		From 6.0pm to 7.0pm programme in support of Infantry operations carried out. Wire in front of IDA TRENCH, MARGARET TRENCH & SOLOMON WAY again engaged.	
	11th to) 16th)		Wire cutting continued each day. During the nights concentrated bursts of fire were fired at intervals on selected objectives within the Group Zone.	

Instructions regarding War Diaries and Intelligence Summaries are contained in F. S. Regs., Part II. and the Staff Manual respectively. Title pages will be prepared in manuscript.

WAR DIARY
or
INTELLIGENCE SUMMARY.
(*Erase heading not required.*)

Army Form C. 2118.

Place	Date	Hour	Summary of Events and Information	Remarks and references to Appendices
X 2 a 5 8	16th	Sept:	During the night the 4 Batteries of the 47th Brigade R.F.A. were withdrawn from the Left Group	
	17th	Sept:	Wire cutting again continued. During the day the 462nd Battery reinforced the Group coming into action in the position vacated by "A"/47 Battery.	
	18th to 28th	Sept:) ")	Wire cutting carried out daily and usual concentrations each night. Hostile Artillery during this period were fairly active against our Battery positions and also back areas.	
	29th	Sept:	Brigade Hd-Qrs relieved by the 179th A.F.A. Bde: and moved to billets vacated by the 179th Brigade in BETHUNE. Command of the Left Artillery Group passed to O.C. 179th Bde: at 10.0am. the Batteries remaining in action under orders of the Left Group.	
	30th	Sept:	Ordinary Brigade Routine carried out including cleaning up and repair of equipment.	
			[signature] Lieut: Col: R.F.A. Commanding 88th Brigade R. F. A.	

A6945 Wt. W11422/M1160 350,000 12/16 D. D. & L. Forms/C./2118/14.

19

Instructions regarding War Diaries and Intelligence Summaries are contained in F. S. Regs., Part II. and the Staff Manual respectively. Title pages will be prepared in manuscript.

WAR DIARY
or
~~INTELLIGENCE SUMMARY.~~
(Erase heading not required.)

Army Form C. 2118.

88 Bde R.F.A. Oct 1917 — 39

Place	Date	Hour	Summary of Events and Information	Remarks and references to Appendices
BETHUNE.	1st		Headquarters 88th Brigade, R.F.A. in reserve at BETHUNE. Batteries still in action under the Command of Officer Commanding 179th (Army) Brigade, R.F.A.	Sheet 36 A SE & sheet 36 SW.
	2nd		" " " " " " " "	
	3rd		" " " " " " " "	
	4th		" " " " " " " "	
LIGNY-LE-GRAND	5th		At 10.00 hours, Headquarters, 88th Bde, RFA. move into ~~action and~~ new reserve position at T 8 d 5 8, the Batteries 88th Bde, RFA still under command of O.C. 179th (Army) Bde, RFA.	
	6th		" " " " " " " "	
	7th		" " " " " " " "	
	8th		" " " " " " " "	
	9th		" " " " " " " "	
	10th		At 2.30.pm. Headquarters 88th Bde, RFA moved to N 30 d 5 5 preparatory to relieving H.Q. 179th (Army) Brigade, R.F.A.	
	11th		At midnight 10/11, Lt.Col. A.T.McGRATH, B.S.C. resumed Command of the Left Artillery Group which comprised 88th Brigade, and 383 and 462 Batteries of the 179th (Army) Brigade, R.F.A. Targets ~~were~~ engaged in O 24 b, c & d, O 30 c & d, O 24 a, c, & b, Farm O 30 c 1 3	

(A9175) Wt W2356/P360 600,000 12/17 D. D. & L. Sch. 52a. Forms/C2118/15.

Army Form C. 2118.

Instructions regarding War Diaries and Intelligence Summaries are contained in F. S. Regs., Par. II. and the Staff Manual respectively. Title pages will be prepared in manuscript.

WAR DIARY
or
INTELLIGENCE SUMMARY.
(Erase heading not required.)

Place	Date	Hour	Summary of Events and Information	Remarks and references to Appendices
N 30 d 5 5	11th	cont.	Cross-roads O 30 d 1 5 and Cross-roads O 30 d 9 8 with good effect.	
	12th		Targets engaged at O 23 d 2 5, O 24 b 95 30, O 24 c 3 8, O 24 c 50 45.	
			Harrassing fire during the night was carried out on road O 30 b 1 3 - P 25 b O 8, Road	
			P 19 a O 2 - P 19 a 8 3, Road O 30 c O 4 - O 30 d 7 6, Road O 30 d 9 8 - P 25 b O 2,	
			Road O 29 b 7 7 - O 24 d O 7, Cross-roads O 30 d 1 6, O 30 b 1 3, O 24 d 40 95.	
	13th		The following targets were engaged. M.G. at O 28 b 45 80, Movement at O 29 d 40 90,	
			Road from O 30 b 1 3 to P 25 b O 8, Road in P 31 c, Road O 30 c O 5 to O 30 d 8 6,	
			Registration was carried out on O 29 d 3 8. Gas bombardment carried out on OPTIC TRENCH.	
			Harrassing fire as usual carried on throughout the night.	
	14th		Targets were engaged as follows:- Movement at House in O 18 c 8 6, wire at O 23 a 4 2,	
			wire at O 23 c 7 5, P 13 d 40 95 (N.F.call) Boche O.P. House in O 17 c, O 30 d 8 7 (N.F.call)	
			During the night special concentration carried out on:- O 23 c 8 3 to O 29 b O 8,	
			O 29 b 1 5 - O 29 b 2 1, O 29 b 2 1 - O 29 d 3 6, O 29 d 3 6,- O 29 d 4 8, Road O 30 b 1 3 -	
			P 25 b O 8, Road P 19 a O 2 - P 19 a 8 3, Road O 30 c O 4 - O 30 d 7 6, Road O 30 d 9 8 -	
			P 25 b O 2, Road O 29 b 7 7 - O 24 d O 7.	
			Special gas bombardment carried out on SUGAR REFINERY in P 31 Central. At each of the	

A6945 Wt. W11422/M1160 35,000 12/16 D. D. & L. Forms/C./2118/14.

Army Form C. 2118.

WAR DIARY
or
~~INTELLIGENCE SUMMARY~~.
(Erase heading not required.)

Instructions regarding War Diaries and Intelligence Summaries are contained in F. S. Regs., Par. II. and the Staff Manual respectively. Title pages will be prepared in manuscript.

Place	Date	Hour	Summary of Events and Information	Remarks and references to Appendices
N 30 d 5	5.14th.		aforementioned concentrations, bursts of fire were employed.	
	15th		88th Brigade, R.F.A. relieved by 74th Divisional Artillery. H.Q. 88th Bde, RFA and Batteries	
			88th Bde, RFA, marched to BETHUNE via LIGNY-LE-GRAND and RUE DE BOIS preparatory to entraining	
	16th.		In Bethune. Usual Brigade routine carried out.	
	17th.		The 88th Bde, RFA entrained at CHOCQUES for FREMICOURT ~~& EXEXXXX~~. HQ/88 detrained at	
			FREMICOURT and marched to CAMBRAI, arriving at the latter place at 5.0.am. 18th Oct.	
	18th.		Batteries of 88th Bde. RFA detrained at FREMICOURT and marched to CAMBRAI, where billets were	Sheet 51A
			taken.	1/40,000
	19th		In billets in CAMBRAI. Cleaning of wagons and harness etc, overhaul, preparatory to moving	
			into action.	
	20th		The Brigade marched to AVESNES LES AUBERT where billets were taken for the night.	
	21st		The Brigade came into action in vicinity of P 35 c. Wagon Lines established in ST.AUBERT,	
			88th Bde, under the administration of the 24th Divisional Artillery.	
	22nd		Registration carried out. Harrassing fire carried out on enemy's communications during	
			the evening.	
	23rd		Batteries of the Brigade fired a barrage in connection with an Infantry Operation.	

A6945 Wt. W11422/M1160 35,000 12/16 D. D. & L. Forms/C./2118/14.

Army Form C. 2118.

Instructions regarding War Diaries and Intelligence Summaries are contained in F. S. Regs., Part II. and the Staff Manual respectively. Title pages will be prepared in manuscript.

WAR DIARY
or
INTELLIGENCE SUMMARY.
(Erase heading not required.)

Place	Date	Hour	Summary of Events and Information	Remarks and references to Appendices
	24th		Barragefired in conjunction with Infantry operation on high ground East of R. ECAILLON	
			viz the line Q 17 - Q 10 - Q 3.	
	25th		Batteries & HQ/88 moved up and occupied positions in vicinity of P 33 d. Batteries silent	
			except for "S.O.S.".	
	26th		Batteries still silent.	
	27th		" " ". HQ/88 moved to SOMMAING.	
	28th		" " "	
	29th		" " "	
	30th		Batteries and HQ/88 moved to vicinity of K 34 a . Registration carried out.	

[signature] Capt for Lieut. Colonel, R. F. A.

4.11.18.

Commanding 88th Brigade, R. F. A.

A6945 Wt. W11422/M1160 350,000 12/16 D. D. & L. Forms/C./2118/14.

126

Instructions regarding War Diaries and Intelligence Summaries are contained in F. S. Regs. Par. II. and the Staff Manual respectively. Title pages will be prepared in manuscript.

WAR DIARY
or
INTELLIGENCE SUMMARY.
(Erase heading not required.)

88th BRIGADE, ROYAL FIELD ARTILLERY.

Army Form C. 2118.

559

Place	Date	Hour	Summary of Events and Information	Remarks and references to Appendices
OUTREBOIS.	1.12.18. to 31.12.18.		Erection of huts for accommodation of personnel, horse standings.	
			Training including:- Instruction in Marching, Saluting and Rifle Drill, Guard Mounting drill, Laying and Fuze Setting, Gas Defence, Signallers visual signalling, also dressed exercises for Gunners and Drivers.	LENS. 1/100,00
			Instruction under the Education Scheme proceeded with. classes held daily with good result.	
			Preparation made for demozilization. Compilation of statistical returns in connection with demobilization.	
			84 men (including coal-miners and pivotal men) despatched to ENGLAND for demobilization.	

W.A. Metcalfe Capt.
for Major, R.F.A.
Commanding 88th Brigade, R.F.A.

www.ingramcontent.com/pod-product-compliance
Lightning Source LLC
Chambersburg PA
CBHW081400160426
43193CB00013B/2078